TEACHING MIXED ABILITY CLASSES

An Individualized Approach

Teaching Mixed Ability Classes

An Individualized Approach

A. V. Kelly

Harper & Row, Publishers

London New York Evanston San Francisco

First published 1974

No part of this book may be used or reproduced in
any manner whatsoever without written permission
except in the case of brief quotations embodied
in critical articles and reviews

Published by Harper & Row Ltd
28 Tavistock Street, London WC2E 7PN

Standard Book Number 06–318024–3 (cloth)
Standard Book Number 06–318015–4 (paper)

Printed in Great Britain by
Richard Clay (The Chaucer Press) Ltd
Bungay, Suffolk

Contents

Introduction

Schools, like all other social institutions, have undergone dramatic changes in the last twenty-five years. A major change in the country's social and educational ideology, accompanied by a large, although by no means adequate, expansion of educational research, has brought about a reorganization of our school system which has resulted in a transformation of the teacher's role. In many ways, life for the teacher in most of our state schools is very different now from what it was even ten years ago. Parents' expectations of him are different; his own objectives are different; his pupils' attitudes are different; his relationship with his pupils is different; the aids available to him are different; and even the composition of his classes has changed drastically.

For perhaps the most striking change that has taken place, certainly the change that has had the most immediate impact on the individual teacher in his own classroom, is the move away from a concern with the selective function of the educational system towards the idea of equality of provision for all children. This ideological change has led to the abolition (albeit only partial in many places) of the $11+$ as a device for selecting children for certain forms of secondary education, the development of the notion of common secondary schooling for all pupils, and the gradual erosion of the view that streaming by ability is the only way to ensure adequate provision for all children. Streaming by ability is now the exception rather than the rule in the organization of primary schools and there is a growing movement away from it in secondary schools.

An increasing number of teachers, then, are finding themselves faced with classes of mixed abilities. This creates particular difficulties for those who have not been prepared, by their training or by their previous experience, to deal with the problems raised or to take advantage of the opportunities offered by this new kind of teaching situation. For quite new methods are needed in teaching classes of this kind. It is sad but true that a great many head teachers have felt that the abolition of streaming in their schools, and the resultant organizational changes, would in themselves bring about equality, progress and all the other ideals they have been motivated by. Unfortunately, the organizational changes can only create the conditions in which teachers can work for these ideals. Changes of organization unaccompanied by changes of method achieve little and sometimes result in a worsening of the situation. I well remember taking a group of trainee-teachers about ten years ago to visit a secondary school which had been among the first to abolish streaming. After a statement from the headmaster of the ideals that had led him to take this step – all of them admirable and quite justified by such research evidence as was available at that time – we were encouraged to tour the school ourselves.

While doing so, I met a friend and ex-colleague who was now on the staff of this school, and received from him a succinct, but perhaps more accurate definition of the new set-up, as, 'a right bloody pantomime'. This, I feel, is fairly typical of what has happened in many schools where a head teacher has decided to make sweeping changes of this kind. Sometimes he has not had the support of his staff, sometimes he has not been aware of the need to ensure that there would be corresponding changes in the approach to the task of education and in the methods adopted by his teachers, (these two, of course, go hand in hand, for without the support of staff any attempt to establish new approaches and new methods will founder); and the result has been disaster for all concerned. As research has indicated, unstreaming will only lead to an improvement in the quality of the education offered by a school if the teachers in that school believe in it and take advantage of the opportunities it offers them to achieve new goals.

Now it is not the purpose of this book to argue the case for or against one or other method of organizing children into teaching units. This has already been done by others. Nor is it the intention to examine the different educational ideologies that are involved in this issue or even the particular form of ideology that lies behind the movement towards unstreaming, although some reference will have to be made to this in order to elucidate some of the principles that will underlie our practice in dealing with mixed ability classes. Rather, in the light of John Dewey's comment that 'while saints are engaged in introspection, burly sinners run the world', the aim is to look at the practicalities of the mixed-ability form of organization, to face the facts that most Primary Schools are now unstreamed, that an increasing number of head teachers of secondary schools are turning to some kind of unstreamed organization, that the introduction of middle schools by many Local Authorities as a result of the recommendation of the Plowden Report is likely to lead to an extension of this kind of situation for 11–13-year-old pupils, that the raising of the school-leaving age may well generate similar mixed-ability groups of 15–16 year olds, and that, as a result of developments of this kind, an increasing number of teachers will be faced by the necessity of changing their approach and methods to cater for the needs of pupils of all abilities. The intention, then, is to offer teachers who find themselves in this kind of situation some guidance at a practical level as to the kind of thing they might plan to do, some suggestions of possibilities they might explore and some indication of the snags that various lines of approach might lead to.

However, teachers cannot be operated by remote-control nor should one try to manipulate them in this way. Practical advice can never take the form of 'chapter and verse' prescription but must attempt to set out the kinds of consideration that should be borne in mind by the individual teacher as he faces up to the task of educating his own pupils in the unique setting of his own classroom, and makes his own professional decisions in relation to their education. In short, practical decisions can only be made from the basis of an adequate understanding of educational theory. Furthermore, one must try to allay the impression that may have been given that the teachers themselves have and should have no say in the way that schools are organized, but must simply adapt their methods to changes brought about by other people. It may be true that at present they often have little say in such developments, although my own experience is that in many cases changes that have been made have been the result of pressures brought to bear on the head teacher by his staff. But it clearly does not follow that it is right for professional people to be denied this kind of control over the conditions in which they practise their profession. Furthermore, as professional people, teachers should have an interest in, and an expert understanding of, the wider aspects of education and the theoretical basis of their own practice. It has long been felt by many people that anyone can teach if he knows the material. One hopes that this myth is sinking into obscurity, but at the same time one feels that in the case of certain kinds of teaching it may well contain more than an element of truth. It must surely never be true, however, that the layman's point of view is as valid as the professional teacher's on the wider issues of educational policy. This is where professional concern, involvement and real expertise should come into their own. If teachers are to exercise control over the forming of educational policy, they will need a thorough grounding in the theoretical bases of education. It must be assumed, therefore, that teachers who may intitially take up this book in order to get some practical help with the tasks that face them in their own classrooms, will also wish to make a careful examination of the theoretical considerations that lie behind the changes they are experiencing. Such an understanding of the theoretical underpinning of new educational policies will both enable them to contribute to what ought to be an ongoing debate on the best methods of educating our young and will enhance their own classroom practice. Therefore, a second aim of this book will be to offer teachers a guide to those developments in educational theory, whether arising from ideology or research, that have led to the changes that are making their professional lives more complicated but potentially more rewarding.

There is no denying that teaching in this kind of situation, although more rewarding, is a much more difficult, demanding and complex job than teaching classes that are relatively homogeneous in terms of ability. However, teachers should not fight shy of it for that reason. One never wants complexity for complexity's sake, but one ought to want to do a professional job and one ought not to be surprised to discover that the satisfactory development of immature and individual minds is a complex task. One hopes that perhaps in time society will come to realize this and accord teachers the kind of professional recognition in every sense of the term that they will have come to deserve. At present, however, few teachers have been trained to meet the complexities of this new situation. If it is a growing movement, as we have suggested, it is clearly necessary that teachers should now be trained to meet it. A third purpose of this book, then, is to suggest ways in which the initial and in-service training of teachers might be modified to prepare them for teaching of this kind.

It is my opinion that these developments, if approached in a positive way, can lead to increased profit on a wide educational front for pupils and to greater rewards for teachers, to a level of job-satisfaction, for example, that has for many been unattainable in a traditional setting. Conversely, if not approached in the right way, it can result in Hell for all concerned. I have worked with teachers whose professional lives were a Hell of this kind and have felt both for them and for their pupils, not only because of the miseries being endured by both, but also because of the opportunities being lost. Education should be a satisfying experience for both teacher and learner. Mixed ability grouping, in my opinion, can make this idea easier to attain. It is the ambition of this book to help teachers towards its attainment.

It is hoped that what is said here will be of value to teachers of mixed-ability classes of all ages and in all kinds of educational institution, since the individual and group work approach advocated seems suited to pupils of all ages, adults no less than children. However, if the emphasis is on the secondary school, this is in part because this seems to be the sector in which teachers are least accustomed to mixed-ability classes at present and most in need of advice on how to tackle them, and also because this is the area of my own experience both as a schoolteacher and as an adviser of trainee teachers. For in many ways this book is the result of work that has been going on at Goldsmiths' College over the last six years. This work has involved tutors and students from almost all departments within the college and many teachers and head teachers from local schools. Its purpose has been to provide the schools with help in curriculum development while at the same time creating a course of training for teachers that would lead to an awareness of the need for and the complexities of continuous curriculum change and the development of some of the skills and understanding that this requires of teachers. Collaboration has been the keynote here and all have worked together towards these common goals. In a sense, therefore, the contribution of all to this book must be acknowledged. Particular thanks are due, however, to certain of my colleagues in the Goldsmiths' College Faculty of Education, to Meriel Downey, Wynne Davies and Pamela Moore for their helpful and constructive comments on the text, to Graham Byrne Hill, who has acted as a sounding-board for each section as it was written and has made encouraging noises and suggestions for improvements in both content and style, and to Bill Bennett and John Ellis for the help they have given from their own particular areas of expertise to the chapters on slow learners and resources respectively. My gratitude must also go to John Handford, Roy Schofield and Arthur Young for their constructive and helpful comments on the first full draft of the text and to the latter in particular for his permission to illustrate a number of points by reference to the work of Conisbrough Northcliffe County High School of which he is headmaster. All have contributed much. None, however, should be held responsible for the views expressed. Even if they share them, I would not wish them to be held to my statement of them. I am sure, however, that they will share my wish that teachers may get from this book both practical advice and an increased understanding of education that will help them to improve their performance in the classroom, to contribute effectively to continued educational development and, as a result, to derive greater satisfaction from their work.

A. V. Kelly
June 1973

Chapter 1

First Principles

Much is being said and written at the present time about the role-conflict that is experienced by many teachers. Such conflict may exist between the teacher's own view of his role and the view he has of what is expected of him by others, by pupils, parents, head teachers, governors, inspectors and others; or it may be that he himself has different views of his role which are incompatible with each other. For example, he may have read and accepted the injunction of many philosophers of education to regard himself as being primarily concerned as an educator to initiate his pupils into worthwhile activities, and he may find this goal difficult to reconcile with the demands of pupils and parents for examination successes or the demand made by his head teacher for firm discipline and control. Research which has been undertaken in this field[1] has indicated, perhaps predictably, that role-conflict is lower among grammar-school teachers, teachers working in schools in largely 'middle-class' areas and teachers of such well-established and obviously necessary and utilitarian subjects as mathematics; it is higher among teachers of less able pupils, teachers employed in 'working-class' areas and teachers of 'low-status' subjects such as domestic science. There seems little doubt, therefore, that changes in educational policy, and particularly changes of the kind we are concerned with here, will tend to increase the teacher's uncertainty about his role and the conflict that can result from this.

It would seem important therefore, at the beginning of any discussion of mixed-ability teaching, to try to be clear about the changes in the teacher's role that are implied by changes of this kind in the organizational structure of the educational system and of individual schools within it. Form should follow function in the designing of social institutions; organization should serve our ends and purposes not create them for us, so that it is not unreasonable to assume that organizational changes of this kind have been and are being implemented because of certain views their authors have about the aims and purposes of education, the type of organizational structure best able to facilitate their achievement and the role of the teacher. There could be no other valid reason for making such changes and creating the resultant uncertainty. Unless teachers are clear about the implications of such organizational changes, they will be unable to adapt their methods to suit the new situation, so that it is important to be clear from the start about what is implied by a move towards an unstreamed form of organization, since to some extent a definite commitment is entailed to particular positions in certain age-old educational controversies.

In the first place, a general point needs to be made concerning the implications for teachers and schools of the social change that has been a

1 See F. Musgrove and P. H. Taylor, *Society and the Teacher's Role* (RKP, 1969), p. 56.

feature of recent years. Rapid technological change has been accompanied by equally dramatic changes in values, in our attitudes to many moral issues; both have resulted in far-reaching changes in our life-style. For the teacher, this means that he must prepare his pupils for a society very different from that in which he grew up himself, but, more importantly, it means that he must prepare them for change itself. In broad terms, it is the teacher's job to develop in children the skills that his society needs, whether they be hunting and fishing or precision tool engineering; it is also his task to hand on to them the values of the society and to initiate them into the traditional culture of the society and the knowledge upon which that culture is based. In all of these areas change in recent years has been so marked that teachers understandably are bewildered as to what skills, values and knowledge they are expected to hand on. If we develop in children the skills that present-day technology requires, we will find that many of these are skills that will become obsolete within their working lives. What is needed, as the Crowther Report[2] stressed, is not a training in particular skills but the development of a general mechanical ability that will make adaptation to the changing requirements of industry a relatively easy matter, a flexibility that will be brought about only if teachers concentrate less on the inculcation of knowledge and more on the acquisition of understanding.

Similarly, in the realm of values there is no one code that the teacher can see it as his job to hand on, no fixed and final goal in this sense for moral education. We live in a pluralist society, a society in which there are many codes of values, and to prepare children for such a society is not to attempt to inculcate a fixed attitude to moral questions but rather to develop in them the ability to think morally and to reach their own conclusions on the ever new moral issues that a changing society will present them with. Again it is flexibility and adaptability that must be the aim and it can be achieved only by a concentration on the acquisition of understanding rather than of knowledge.

Finally, in the realm of knowledge itself, what is needed in an age of computers is not people who can store it, but people who can use it intelligently and contribute to its continued expansion. In all of these spheres it is clear that the teacher can no longer be merely a conservative agent for the transmission of traditional skills, values and knowledge; he must set about providing children with the abilities that will ensure continued development on all of these fronts. He must look to the future rather than to the past.

The second preliminary point that needs to be stressed is that developments of this kind imply no reduction in the importance of the teacher's role as instructor. There is no reason to assume that less emphasis needs to be placed on learning or on intellectual achievement in a situation where the aim is flexibility of this kind and where the mixed ability group is the basic teaching unit. Sociologists[3] have distinguished between the 'expressive'

2 *15 to 18* (HMSO, 1959).
3 See F. Musgrove, *British Journal of Educational Psychology*, 1966.

and 'instrumental' functions of the school, between its social and pastoral responsibilities and its duty to promote study. Clearly, this distinction is important, but it is often too readily assumed that this can be the basis for distinguishing the primary from the secondary school, the secondary modern from the grammar school, the education of 'working-class' pupils from that of 'middle-class' pupils and the ideals of the College of Education from those of the University department of education. Too readily it is assumed that the main objective of the primary and of the secondary modern school is the social welfare of its pupils and that their intellectual advancement is of secondary importance; too often it is assumed that Colleges of Education, preparing teachers mainly for primary and non-selective secondary schools, will stress the social and pastoral role of the teacher to the detriment of his duties as an instructor; too frequently it is assumed that a teacher who evinces a concern for the social welfare of his pupils is *ipso facto* ignoring their intellectual needs.

As a result of this rather naïve dichotomy, there is a tendency to assume that the main purpose of a teacher of a mixed-ability group should be social, pastoral, 'expressive'. There is no justification whatsoever for this assumption. The advent of the mixed-ability class will, of course, make it necessary for him to take a broader view of his duties and recognize the need to include such considerations in making provision for his pupils. He must begin to look at the curriculum not only from the point of view of certain logical requirements of the subject-matter, but also in the light of the psychological and social requirements of his pupils and must accept responsibility for their moral, social and emotional as well as their intellectual development. If he does this, he will soon realize that it is not possible in practice to distinguish these, since there is an interrelationship between learning and feeling, between the cognitive and the affective, that cannot be ignored if he is to attend successfully to either need. However, there is no reason why the introduction of a mixed ability organization to a school should bring with it any reduction in intellectual rigour or in the academic demands to be made by teachers of their pupils. The teacher's prime job is to teach and this is not altered by this kind of organizational change, whose purpose rather is to enable him to teach more effectively. It is *how* he is to teach that is changed and we must turn our attention to what is implied for that.

All the implications for changes in the approach to teaching required in a mixed-ability class derive from the fact that such a class is by definition heterogeneous. It is a well-known, although usually disregarded, fact that all classes are heterogeneous, even in situations where the streaming is very fine. Nevertheless, for economy's sake, teachers have tended to ignore this fact, to regard streamed classes as homogeneous and to teach their classes as units, 'aiming at the middle' and dealing with the 'top' and 'bottom' as best as they can. No teacher faced with a mixed-ability class can hope to keep up this kind of approach for long. 'Top' and 'bottom' will be too far apart. It will be necessary, therefore, for him to view his class as a collection of individuals and to recognize individual differences of all kinds. Although psychologists have been stressing the importance of individual differences for education for forty years or more, they have tended to be largely concerned only with differences of intellectual ability and teachers in practice have tended to follow suit. Differences in rates of progress and in amounts of material that can readily be assimilated have been taken fully into account by all concerned with education – this after all is the justification for streaming and selection; it has been accepted that children will progress at different speeds and that for some the work will need to be watered down, sometimes to a very thin gruel; but no other differences have been regarded as educationally significant. If they are not significant, there can be little justification for doing away with streaming, other than perhaps on social grounds, since streaming is designed to enable teachers to cope most efficiently with different speeds of learning and different points of cut-off in a situation where all children are to learn the same and to proceed along the one educational highway as far as their intellectual fuel will carry them. To make away with grading of this kind implies a wish to take account of more subtle differences between individual children and a conviction that the content of education must be varied to suit individual needs. In other words, to abandon streaming, to embrace from choice the clearly heterogeneous teaching group is to make a commitment to the notion of individualized or personalized learning, to providing for each child according to his or her unique educational requirements. This is what many have meant by the expression 'child-centred' education. 'Learner-centred', 'individual-centred' or 'person-centred' might be better terms, since too often 'child-centred' has rather naïvely been taken to imply a 'mothering' approach and little more. What many 'child-centred' theorists have been advocating for a long time is that educational provision should be adapted to the individual pupil. In the mixed-ability class this becomes essential and its implications need to be looked at in some detail.

In the first place, there are quite serious implications here for the content of education. There was a time when all discussions of curriculum centred on decisions concerning its content. This is why such discussions did not get very far; they were fundamentally mistaken in that they equated content with goals or objectives, or rather their concern with content blinded them to questions concerning goals or objectives. To plan a curriculum, then, was to set out a programme of content, and inevitably such curricula were planned for groups rather than for individuals. Recent work in the field of curriculum study has highlighted questions of objectives and has rightly seen these questions as being central to curriculum planning and logically prior to questions of content or method. Decisions about the content and methods of education can only be taken when we have achieved a clear view of our educational objectives.[4] Whatever the source of these objectives, whether they are socially determined or derived in some way from an

4 For a full discussion of this and related points see P. H. Hirst and R. S. Peters, *The Logic of Education* (RKP, 1970).

analysis of the notion of education itself, we must be clear about them before we can consider any of the other questions that face us as curriculum planners.

We must recognize, of course, that in practice there will always be a significant difference between our intentions and our actual achievements, not least because our pupils' objectives and those of their parents will differ from our own, and that our own objectives will be modified by our practical experiences; but curriculum planning is essential if education is to be a purposeful activity and it is objectives that constitute both the central and the common element in such planning. Once we concentrate our attention on them, we can see the secondary status of content, we can see that what is important is not that we should strive to ensure that all children assimilate a certain body of knowledge, but that we should be endeavouring to lead them to the same educational goals; and there may be as many roads to these goals as there are individual children. What matters is not that all children should have a knowledge of the main events of the French Revolution but that they should all be able to think historically and have a developing understanding of the problems that beset man's attempts to learn to live with his fellows; not that they should all 'know' Boyle's Law, but that they should all be able to think scientifically and understand how man's knowledge of his physical environment has been and is being developed; not that they should all have learnt Hamlet's soliloquy, but that they should have been introduced to and brought to value literature which is capable of interpreting and enriching human life.

However, if we accept that the *objectives* of the curriculum are the same for all children, it is not necessary to assume that the *content* must be the same for all. This has been the mistake of the past. We have attended only to intellectual differences in our pupils, as we have seen, and have been prepared to modify only the rate of progress we expected of them or the amount of content we expected them to digest. In doing so, we have pretended we were individualizing our approach – the growing use of teaching machines is welcomed by some as an individualizing of learning in this very limited sense – but this is far too unsophisticated and is, in fact, a largely illusory form of individualization. If we accept that only the objectives of education are common, we must be prepared for quite dramatic differences of content and method to suit the dramatic differences that clearly exist in children's styles of learning, interests, backgrounds, ambitions and the many other facets of their unique personalities. Many teachers have, of course, tried very hard to adapt their approach to the needs of individual pupils, but the system has too often made difficulties for them. The advent of the mixed-ability group should have helped to remove some of these difficulties, but it can only succeed if teachers themselves can shake off some of their preconceptions concerning the content of education and move towards a greater clarity of thinking about the curriculum. Once they have freed themselves of the limitations imposed by this narrow view of content, they can take advantage of the greater scope for manoeuvre that a mixed-ability group provides and the greater opportunities to adapt both content and method to the individual.

A second point about content arises naturally from what has just been said. Just as we can no longer justify a belief that the content of education should be the same for all pupils, so we can no longer assume a unique sequence of learning even for the same material. There are no grounds for the assumption that all knowledge is organized hierarchically, that children must be taken through it step by step or, to change the metaphor, that they must build their knowledge brick by brick. This is another example of the folklore that has for too long hindered the establishment of a serious theoretical basis for the practice of education. Too readily it has been assumed that children cannot learn 'y' until they have learnt 'x', or that certain 'subjects' cannot be broached before certain others have been begun, or that certain kinds of topic cannot be tackled before a certain age has been reached. To some extent the work of psychologists such as Piaget and Kohlberg on the development of children's thinking has reinforced this kind of view, but perhaps their findings have been interpreted with too little sophistication. Again there is a confusion of ends and means. Their work would certainly seem to suggest that there is a definite sequence to the acquisition by children of certain kinds of concept, and therefore that there are certain psychological considerations to be taken into account in curriculum planning. It does not follow that there exist psychological factors which rigidly control the sequence in which we must present pupils with the content of their education. A great deal more work needs to be done in this area, but in the meantime it would seem safer to assume, with Jerome Bruner, that anything can be taught to any child at any age in an intellectually honest fashion; that it *is* possible to devise versions of any subject that will make it suitable for presentation to pupils at any age or stage of development, if for other reasons it seems warranted. The same material can and should be presented again later in a different way so that gradually the conceptual progress we are after can be attended to and our educational objectives achieved. This process of covering the same ground again and again at different levels of complexity Bruner calls the 'spiral curriculum'.[5] It is a notion that is worth a great deal of careful attention.

A third and final point to be made here about the implications of these changes in approach for the content of education is that it would seem that in such a situation traditional subject barriers must lose some of their strength. Again this might appear *prima facie* to be flying in the face of logic, denying the validity of the logical differences that clearly exist between the disciplines. Again, to a large extent, all we are flying in the face of is folklore and again it is a folklore that has confused ends and means. Our objective may be and should be to get pupils on the inside of certain distinct forms of knowledge, but there is no evidence to suggest that the only or even the best means of achieving this objective is by organizing

5 J. Bruner, *The Process of Education* (Harvard UP, 1960) and *Towards a Theory of Instruction* (Harvard UP, 1966).

the curriculum into separate subject areas. It has been argued that the best way to achieve this objective and at the same time to ensure that links between subjects are not ignored is to establish a curriculum which is 'fundamentally subject-based, but which pursues links between the different disciplines with real seriousness'.[6] It is being argued here that the logic of the mixed-ability class makes it necessary to approach the problem from the other end, to ensure that pupils are made aware of logical differences between disciplines as they pursue their individual programmes. Once again much work needs to be done in this area, but once again we would be well advised not to prejudge the issue. Our main concern as teachers is to discover the most efficient means of leading individual pupils towards our educational objectives and we must not without good reason let ourselves be restricted in our decisions by other considerations.

Let us now turn to a consideration of the implications of the mixed-ability teaching situation for teaching method. Clearly, what we have said about individualizing content will apply to method; methods, like content, should be adapted to the learning styles of individual pupils and we will look in detail later at the practical implications of this. However, there is one general point about method that needs to be made at this stage since as a general principle it will inform all our practice. It will be a basic rule of our approach to learning and teaching in this kind of situation that we must lean towards heuristic rather than didactic methods. This point is made here not from ideological considerations nor as logically entailed by positions we have already accepted but as a point of sheer practical necessity. If we accept the view that every pupil must be helped to advance at his own pace by his own route to the goals of education, then, unless we assume a much more favourable pupil–teacher ratio than is ever possible or even desirable, we must conclude that there are real limitations on the time a teacher can spend 'teaching' any one pupil and that of practical necessity each must learn to work on his own. It is in my view a mistake to make a great thing of 'discovery methods', to talk rather loosely about 'learning to learn' and so on, not least because it creates another dichotomy to add to the many that litter educational theory, most of which arise from a lack of subtlety in our thinking. We ought not to be asking whether instruction or discovery based methods are more appropriate in education and thus generating an artificial conflict between the two; our energies ought to be directed towards discovering what combinations of the two approaches are most effective and under what conditions. The education of a person is neither an imposition on him from without nor a natural development from within; it is a combination of the two as the growing, developing individual reacts to his environment. As teachers, therefore, we ought not to be torn asunder by asking ourselves whether we should 'teach' our pupils or let them 'find out' things for themselves. It is impossible to learn anything without both of these elements. We ought to be experi-

6 See P. H. Hirst in Schools Council Working Paper no. 12, *The Educational Implications of Social and Economic Change* (HMSO), p. 83.

menting with both approaches, remembering that the most effective combination for each pupil will depend on his own style of learning. Is it best to give him a few facts and some clear indications of how he can go beyond them on his own or does he need to be fed a lot of straight factual information? These are the questions teachers should be asking themselves as they plan the work of individual pupils. There will be occasions, even in mixed-ability classes, when some straight class teaching will be appropriate, but for the most part in this kind of situation 'teaching' will mean organizing the learning of individual pupils, and they must of necessity work for much of the time on their own or in small sub-groups.

Nor is it necessary to assume that we should organize our programme in two parts, one devoted to the pursuit of interests and individual projects, the other to the acquisition of 'basic skills', as is done in many primary schools. Such skills cannot be taught at anything other than a basic level in isolation from the disciplines of which they are an essential part,[7] so that teachers must be aware of the need to develop these skills through the interests and individual projects of pupils in much the way that many infant teachers set about the teaching of reading, writing and number.

A corollary of this insistence on individualizing education is that the pupil is being asked to take an increased and ever-increasing responsibility for his own learning. This is as it should be, since if we are concerned to educate, then part of what it means to be educated is to be autonomous, to be self-propelled. If our pupils learn everything under duress and compulsion, they may in the end be very knowledgeable but they will never be educated. Furthermore, as we have seen, the changing nature of society makes autonomy a vital economic aim of education, since a changing society needs autonomous citizens. Thus practical necessity is here the ally of our educational ideals. If education is our concern, then one of our objectives must be the autonomy of the learner. From the beginning we must be trying to create a situation in which our pupils' learning is increasingly self-directed and self-propelled, until eventually that education can go on without us; we become superfluous. It is the educator's job to render his own services unnecessary.

There are, of course, a number of difficulties inherent in this approach to education. To begin with, it will be apparent that pupils from 'working-class' backgrounds are unlikely to take naturally to this method of learning. A facility with language is required for learning of this kind that many recent studies have suggested the 'working-class' child does not have. A pupil whose conversation at home is confined within a restricted code of language[8] is bound to find it more difficult to engage in self-propelled learning. Some kind of elaborated code may be acquired through education, but it will perhaps never be 'natural' and its acquisition will require a great deal of direct personal contact with a teacher. The social climate of those homes with a tendency towards somewhat authoritarian and

7 ibid.
8 See B. B. Bernstein, *Educational Research*, 1961.

arbitrary relationships also is likely to breed dependence rather than independence of thought within the child,[9] and therefore will not promote the child's ability to take responsibility for his own work in school. How much easier is it for pupils from 'middle-class' homes? Certainly it must be somewhat easier, since many of the disadvantages just mentioned will be absent, but it can never be entirely easy for anyone. The solution, however, cannot be the rejection of this approach. We cannot reject it since, as we have seen, the very logic of education forces us to accept it and so much of the work of educationists in recent years has revealed it as the only basis for learning. What we need to do is to accept self-direction as an aim but to realize that with all pupils its achievement will be a slow process and with some a very slow process indeed. Much of the pupil's work, especially in the early stages, will need to be teacher-directed, but the aim throughout will be eventual self-direction. Again much more work must be done to help teachers with the practicalities of leading their pupils towards this goal. Some of these practicalities we will look at in later chapters. For the present it is sufficient that we make the goal explicit and stress what was stressed earlier, that no loss of rigour is entailed. If the self-directed learning degenerates into self-directed playing or messing around, if the rigour and the learning disappear, then we are as far from achieving our objectives as we are when we take a highly didactic stance from the outset.

Let us finally turn to a consideration of the implications of these changes for the role of the teacher and the conditions under which he does his job. For many reasons, both social and historical, the teacher in the British-maintained school has tended, consciously or not, to see his job as being concerned mainly with the promotion of the able pupil rather than encouraging the progress of all his charges. Historically, education in Britain has been a privilege granted to an increasingly large proportion of the populace (in contrast to the United States, for example, where it has for long been every child's democratic right upheld by the community), and British society has long been dominated by elitism rather than equality and an emphasis on what sociologists call the ascription of roles rather than their achievement (again in contrast to the United States where it has long been believed that status should not be ascribed by some criterion such as birth but should be achieved by individual ability).[10] For a long time, therefore, many British teachers have tended to emphasize their selective and elitist role, the teacher in the primary school, for example, concentrating on the allocation of children to different types of secondary school, the secondary-school teacher concentrating on passing pupils on to various forms of higher education or into various types of occupation. The move towards mixed-ability grouping implies a move towards equality and the achievement of roles, and the teacher's role must change accordingly. In a

9 See J. Klein, *Samples from English Cultures* (RKP, 1965).

10 See S. M. Lipset, *The First New Nation* (Heinemann, 1964) and E. Hoyle, *The Role of the Teacher* (RKP, 1969).

situation where learning is being individualized, where all pupils are not pursuing the same work in competition with each other but pursuing their own paths to learning, the teacher must renounce his selective, elitist role and accept responsibility for the educational advance of all his pupils on a broad front. This is perhaps the greatest professional reorientation that is required of him by these changes.

Secondly, an increased responsibility falls on him for decisions about the content of education. The teaching profession in Britain has always enjoyed a high level of autonomy in the matter of curriculum content and, because of the nature of his work, the individual member of the profession has also had a high degree of autonomy in this field. Inspectors, advisers, the Schools Council and other bodies can, and do, offer advice, comment and suggestion, but in the end it is the head teachers, the heads of departments and the assistant teachers themselves who decide what the content of the curriculum will be. When the emphasis in curriculum planning is on content, they can do much of this collectively, but when content is individualized, as we have suggested it must be in the mixed-ability group, a great deal more responsibility devolves on the individual teacher. He must be prepared to make many more decisions concerning what is appropriate for individual pupils in the light of their unique needs and the overriding objectives of education. Like his pupils, he himself must become far more self-propelled. In my view, this entitles him to 'danger money', since such decisions are far-reaching and crucial to the lives of many individuals.

Thirdly, it will probably be apparent that in a classroom where learning of the kind we are describing is going on, there will be far greater informality than in a classroom where the teacher's main offering is the formal lesson. Where each child is doing his own thing, there must be a relatively informal atmosphere. This creates a situation which is far more demanding for the teacher. Apart from the demands that it makes on his intellectual resources and methodological expertise, it is a situation in which a completely different pattern of authority exists. The teacher must be *an* authority rather than rely on the fact (sometimes a somewhat doubtful fact) that he is *in* authority; his authority must be earned since it cannot be given to him and to earn it in this kind of situation is no easy task. There is already some evidence[11] to suggest that it places a much higher premium on the teacher's personal qualities. It certainly makes heavy demands on his skill as a teacher and on the relationships he is able to develop with his pupils.

It is not the aim of this book to tell teachers how they can develop their personal qualities but a great deal can be done to improve basic techniques in a very practical way and to help with the development of teacher–pupil relationships. Now that we have some general idea of the principles that underlie mixed-ability teaching, we can turn to a detailed examination of the practical arrangements that may lead to such improvements.

11 See F. Musgrove and P. H. Taylor, op. cit., p. 24.

Chapter 2

Individual and Group Assignments

Panaceas are as difficult to find in education as they are in any other sphere and there is no one answer that can be given to the question, 'How do I set about teaching my mixed-ability class?' Every child differs in important respects from every other, so does every class, every school, every neighbourhood, as well as every teacher and head teacher, so that the approach to education must be adapted to the particular conditions that apply in any one situation at any one time. Every school and every teacher will and should develop an individual style and deal with a unique situation in a way peculiarly appropriate to it. It is the sameness of so much secondary education that makes one wonder how it can be satisfactory for so many different pupils. In any attempt to present an overall view of what is entailed by an individualized approach to education, therefore, there is the ever-present danger of encouraging the growth of a new orthodoxy, a new gospel, which may soon become just as restrictive as the old and may prove just as effective in limiting the innovatory role of individual teachers or groups of teachers. This must be avoided at all costs, since the education of all our children can only be forwarded by placing more responsibility for it in the hands of the teachers who are in personal contact with them. We have suffered for too long from education by remote-control. It is, however, possible to offer teachers some guidelines as to how they might set about this kind of teaching, to offer them some tools which may enable them to do their job to their own greater satisfaction. To provide a carpenter with a chisel is not to tell him how to use it nor in any way to limit his creativity; rather it is to widen his scope and extend the range of his opportunities. It is in that spirit that the practical suggestions which follow are offered.

A second preliminary point is that these suggestions are offered with the aim not of replacing existing techniques but rather of supplementing them. For example, it is sometimes felt that once streaming is abandoned class teaching must also cease, that the teacher should at no stage be seen teaching his class as a whole. This again springs from too unsophisticated a view of the teacher's task. There is no evidence to suggest that class teaching is always ineffective when used with mixed-ability classes. Many teachers still make use of it most effectively. Some indeed are concerned about the implications of group or individual methods, since these can lead to the accentuation of individual differences and the aggravation of precisely those social disadvantages that unstreaming is concerned to avoid.[1] Class teaching then, still has its part to play in the teaching of mixed-ability groups; indeed, there may be occasions when a lecture or other such presentation

1 See, for example, M. Hardie (ed.), *At Classroom Level* (PSW Educational, 1971), pp. 34–5.

to a whole year group of pupils will be appropriate. If the emphasis in what follows is placed on group and individual teaching methods, it is because these are relatively new to many teachers so that it is here that practical advice is needed. They are suggested, however, as additional teaching devices that will add flexibility to the teacher's approach and not as new methods advocated to oust the old and tried.

Finally, it must be stressed that what is discussed here should be seen as having relevance and point for the work of any teacher in any classroom. Individual and group methods can be used to effect with streamed as well as with unstreamed classes, within subjects as well as in general teaching or interdisciplinary situations, in schools where the general approach is formal as well as in those where new methods are being tried. Clearly, the teacher who wishes to work in this way will find it easier to do so in a school where the organizational structure is designed to promote this kind of approach; where, for example, the timetable provides him with the substantial blocks of time needed to develop this kind of work rather than the short 30–40-minute periods which give too little time for individual or group work. But it is not impossible for him to work in this way even in a school that is not planned with this approach in mind. Similarly, although, as we shall see, there are considerable advantages to be gained from organizing much of this work on a team-teaching basis, the individual teacher whose school does not provide him with such an opportunity need not feel that there is nothing he can do himself. The practical suggestions which follow, although directed primarily at those teachers whose work involves them with mixed-ability groups, should be seen as having relevance for all teachers regardless of the type of teaching situation they are in.

Our main concern is with the techniques of the individual or group assignment and the first question that arises is that of how to decide on the content of such assignments. As in most areas of educational decision, one can find almost a complete spectrum of answers to this question, from those who would say that content is not affected and that it is method only that is changed, so that common syllabuses for all pupils will still need to be planned in advance, to those who would place no limitation at all on the activity of pupils but would allow them complete freedom of choice in what they wish to do and learn. The answer that each teacher gives to this question will depend on the particular circumstances in which he finds himself and on the view he takes of the wider purposes of education and of his own objectives within that context. Let us consider the two extreme positions in a little more detail.

The teacher who is required to work to a detailed syllabus will have little choice in this matter anyway. For him the objectives of his teaching are assigned and, while he can gain much from the methodological advantages that the mixed-ability group and the individual or group assignment approach can offer, there is little for him in the opportunities such a set-up provides for rethinking the purposes of education. Similarly, the teacher who may have much more freedom of action than this but whose view of education is such as to lead him to see educational goals in terms of subject-matter will want to preplan a syllabus for his classes, whether in a particular subject area or in a combination of subject areas. At this end of the spectrum, then, traditional syllabuses, perhaps revamped in an attempt to achieve integration of subject areas, will provide an answer to the question of the content of individual or group assignments. It was argued in chapter 1 that such an approach loses many of the advantages of the mixed-ability set-up, but it is still perhaps the most usual situation, even in second-ary schools that have changed to a mixed-ability pattern of organization, and what will be said soon about method is as relevant to this as to any looser situation.

At the other end of the spectrum is the teacher who is left to himself in the classroom and elects to give his pupils a similar degree of freedom. It may be argued that such a teacher is avoiding the issue of content every bit as much as the one who relies on a syllabus. It would certainly be ar-gued by many, again as we suggested in chapter 1, that such an approach is based on a misunderstanding of education, a conceptual confusion of education with other related but very different notions such as 'growth' and 'maturation'. However, to argue thus might be to miss the point, since a teacher who approached his work in this open-ended way might wish to reply that, far from avoiding the issue of content, he is interpreting it in a highly individualistic manner, and that, far from confusing education with growth or maturation, he has a very clear view of education as intimately connected with the individuality of each pupil, that in fact he makes not one but many decisions on content as he approves, modifies or disapproves the choices of areas for study made by each of his pupils. Clearly, much depends on the degree of freedom given to the pupils and the way in which the individual teacher handles the situation; it is not the absence of a pre-planned syllabus in itself which lays one open to these charges. One criticism, however, must be applied to this approach generally and that is that it creates a job for Superman. No mortal teacher is, or can be, equipped to deal adequately or successfully with what is likely to come up if thirty pupils of whatever age are encouraged to work on their own in this un-limited way. One has only to think of the endless stream of questions that flows from any small child to realize what is likely to result from encoura-ging pupils to explore freely those things that interest them. If we also remember the greater age, experience and range of interests of secondary pupils, my point will be more than clear.

Aware of this problem and also of the opportunities that would be lost if clear statements of content were drawn up in advance, many teachers have chosen the theme approach as one that gives most of the advantages of the free situation but protects them from a crippling variety of demands. A broad area of work is selected and pupils are offered a range of choices within that area. It is felt that this kind of approach has advantages for the pupil also in so far as, if the theme is well chosen, he can see his work in a context which is broader than the immediate task confronting him but not so broad as to be entirely beyond his own horizon. The main purpose of a theme, then, is to provide a framework in which both teacher and pupil can work securely, profitably and successfully.

Choice of the right theme is, therefore, of crucial importance. A theme which is too narrow, 'The Earth Worm' for example, will defeat the purposes of this approach since it will not be a theme at all; it will be a statement of content like a syllabus and will provide little freedom of manoeuvre for teacher or pupil. On the other hand, it is equally unsatisfactory to go to the other extreme and choose a theme which is so general as to provide no real framework at all. A theme like 'Man and His World', for example, is again no theme at all since it is hardly definitive and does not do for teacher or pupil the very thing a theme should do, namely to delimit the area of their work. A good theme will be one which will provide teacher and pupil with both a structure and as much freedom as each can tolerate.

To provide a coherent structure for the work of teacher and pupils, a theme must be a theme in the full sense of the term. There must be a unity to all that is studied under the label of any particular theme and that unity must be based on a logical rather than a contingent association of those subjects or areas of enquiry that are being subsumed under this particular heading. If we do not hold on to this as a basic principle, then the idea of a theme loses all point, since there will no longer be any coherence either within the separate areas of the individual pupil's own work or between his work and that of his fellows. To use a theme as the basis of a programme of any kind entails a concern for giving the work of all pupils this kind of coherence and point. To take as a theme 'Hands', for example, and to allow this to be explored through biology (the physical structure of hands), industrial sociology (working with one's hands) and religious studies (the 'laying on of hands'), or to allow the theme 'Water' to lead to a study of H_2O, water transport and water melons is to miss the point of this kind of approach to education and to introduce a random element and a lack of coherence – or worse, a false and misleading semblance of coherence – into pupils' work that is hardly consonant with what most of us understand by education. The main purpose of a theme, then, is to provide an intelligible, coherent and logical context for the work of all pupils.

Several further factors must be borne in mind when a theme is being chosen. The ages, interests, aptitudes and abilities of the pupils concerned must clearly be a prime concern. A theme must provide pupils with scope for work of a kind they can cope with and profit from. A second important consideration must be the competences of the teacher – or of the team of teachers, if this approach is being used in conjunction with team-teaching. It would be very foolish of a teacher to select a theme which required him to break new ground on almost every front to cope with all that pupils might want to work on within the theme and to take advantage of the opportunities it might offer to further their education. Thirdly, a theme should be chosen with a clear view of the objectives that it is hoped will be achieved by it. A theme is essentially a vehicle for teaching and should not be regarded merely as a means of keeping idle hands busy, although this is, of course, another important consideration. Finally, regard must be paid to the local conditions that prevail in the school and its neighbourhood. There is little point in selecting a theme which will generate a lot of practical activity in a school which is very short of workshop facilities nor in undertaking to work on 'The Lower Thames and its Environs' with a group of pupils who live in Glasgow. All of these factors and many others that will quickly spring to the mind of the experienced teacher must be kept much to the fore when selecting an area of enquiry for a class of pupils.

Once a theme is chosen, the next decision that must be made is whether all the pupils will work on the same things and engage in the same activities or whether they will be allowed to choose their own field of study and devote their attention to that. This decision will depend primarily on the objectives it is hoped the scheme will achieve. It may be felt, for example, that our objective will best be achieved if every pupil is required to look at the theme from a number of different points of view and to experience all or several of the activities planned. Some of the Nuffield science projects are good examples of this kind of approach. A theme such as 'Mass' might have as its objectives the development of an understanding of several related concepts such as those of weight, volume and specific gravity. If this is the aim, then it might be argued that it will best be achieved by taking each pupil through a 'circus' of experiments, which enable him to experience the problems of weighing and measuring a variety of solids, liquids and possibly gases also and to examine the relationships between the data he thus acquires. Similarly, a history teacher might set up an exploration of Norman England by requiring all pupils to work in turn on the details of the Battle of Hastings, the armour and weapons in use at the time, the castles, the Domesday Book, monasteries, feudalism, the open-field system and so on, and by arranging for these separate enquiries to be related to each other in such a way as to build up for each pupil a clear picture of the age. In this kind of situation, where the 'circus' approach is regarded as the best method of achieving one's aims, this stage of preparation requires the careful planning of each of the activities or areas of study seen as essential to the achievement of the whole and of the means of bringing them together. Once this has been done, the problem of content has been solved.

However, it may be felt that what is needed is to encourage each pupil to pursue in depth only one or two aspects of the theme, to share his findings or the findings of his group with the others in his class and to see other aspects of the theme by looking at the work of other individuals or groups. A theme such as 'Communications' – a very popular theme in situations where an interdisciplinary approach is being deliberately fostered – is one where it is felt that the teacher's objectives can be achieved, that children can be helped to see the point and can come to understand the importance and relevance of communications in human development by each exploring one or two aspects only, provided that they are given plenty of real opportunities to share their findings with each other and can thus see the many different sides to the concept. Some may be led by their interests into approaching the topic from an historical point of view and working on the history of the development of roads, canals, railways or sea-transport; others may prefer to consider the geographical problems that are involved; others still may be drawn to an exploration of the scientific aspects of communication, the development of the telegraph, telephone, radio or television, as well as of various forms of mechanical propulsion; another group may wish to consider some of the implications of improved standards of communication for man's moral and social life; and there is much scope for yet another group to consider language as a form of communication or non-verbal communication through the arts. In this way, each pupil can have the benefit of working to some depth in the area that is of most direct interest to him while gaining some view of the breadth of the theme by seeing what his or her colleagues are doing. Clearly, this approach creates a much looser situation than the 'circus' approach and the teacher has now many individual decisions to take concerning the proposed content of each pupil's or each group's line of enquiry. Many lines he will be able to foresee and to think about and plan for in advance, but it is always possible and often happens that pupils will themselves come up with suggestions that are as good as any he has thought of and these will need to be assessed on the spot.

On what criteria should decisions of this kind be made? In the first place, we should not forget that one of the main arguments in favour of this kind of approach is that working through pupils' own interests brings great gains in motivation and that the best way of getting pupils to work is to allow them to work on things that interest them. Psychologists, such as Piaget,[2] who have concentrated their attention on a study of intellectual development, have stressed the importance of intrinsic motivation, of work done for its own sake rather than for some extrinsic reason, in encouraging and promoting intellectual development. This is clearly also the kind of motivation we should be seeking if we are concerned with education in the full sense of the term, since to be educated one must have come to value that education for its own sake. Intrinsic motivation, however, must be sought in the pupil and not in the content of what is offered to him or the methods we adopt in our teaching of him. Intrinsic motivation can only be achieved if we allow a pupil to select his own work and to become absorbed in it.

However, much play is made in theoretical discussions of education of the fact that what a pupil is interested in is not necessarily the same thing as what is in his interests,[3] that some interests children and young people

2 For a full discussion of this point, see D. Elkind, *Children and Adolescents* (OUP, 1970), pp. 130–32.
3 See, for example, R. F. Dearden, *The Philosophy of Primary Education* (RKP, 1968), pp. 18 ff.

have may need to be positively discouraged and that education involves more than pursuing hobbies and requires a breadth of experience greater than is encompassed by the interests of the average pupil. The dangers of merely catering for the interests of each pupil, therefore, are firstly that his interests may be such that we would regard the pursuit of them to be miseducative, if not positively harmful, and secondly that, even where this does not apply, merely to pursue interests one already has may be to miss out on many things that we would see as being constitutive of an education in the full sense of the term. This could be particularly to the disadvantage of the pupil whose home provides him with a limited cultural background and, therefore, a restricted range of interests.

It must be stressed again, as it was in chapter 1, that while accepting the motivational value of working through pupils' interests, teachers must be prepared to make firm decisions about what these interests lead their pupils to undertake. The objectives that we have in planning work even in this kind of free situation must be kept in mind when evaluating proposed lines of enquiry, as must the need for these enquiries to satisfy the demands for coherence we have already discussed. We must, of course, be prepared to consider these objectives in relation to what we know about individual pupils. We may feel, for example, that a great deal has been achieved if we have produced even a spark of interest from certain pupils and that they should be allowed to do what they want to do merely on the grounds that they will thus derive the satisfaction of doing something. On the whole, however, decisions of this kind must be made in the light of what we consider to be worthwhile activities and what we consider likely to lead towards the goals we have in mind. Furthermore, pupils will tend to be interested in the superficially more attractive aspects of a topic and will need to be led into those aspects which are less exciting but which may be necessary to give coherence to the whole and to promote understanding. If education is to mean anything it must involve the extension and development of pupils' interests rather than the mere satisfaction of them. It may be true that what is worthwhile can only be defined in terms of what is worthwhile to the pupil, but if the teacher is to play any positive role in education, it must be by his or her skill at developing the potential of the individual pupil revealed through his interests rather than merely feeding those interests in the way that anyone with an adequate supply of paper, paint and other materials might do. What is being argued is that the pupil has a right to contribute to the discussion of his own education, not that he is not competent to decide entirely for himself its content, methods or objectives. It is the failure to realize this and the resulting involvement of many pupils in totally undirected activity that has led to most of the criticisms that have been made of 'free' methods in schools.

With objectives clearly thought out, a theme chosen as a likely means to the achievement of those objectives and decisions of content made or at least principles established upon which they will be made, the teacher's next problem is to put all of this into action. We must now turn, therefore, to a discussion of some methods that might prove helpful to the teacher adopting an individual or group assignment approach.

The first task in any educational undertaking is to get the right psychological 'set', to arouse interest, to ensure motivation, so that the teacher must begin by trying to communicate to all of his pupils the interest that it is hoped he himself already has in the project he has planned and to show them that there is something of interest and value in it for everyone. There are several ways in which this can be attempted.

Many teachers favour the 'impact session', the 'key' or 'lead' lesson, as the most effective method of arousing interest. The new work is introduced to the pupils by a presentation of as stimulating and exciting a kind as can be devised. Clearly, there are advantages here in having a team of teachers involved, but there is a great deal that the individual teacher can do with his own class. Films, audio- or video-tapes, film-strips and other such aids will obviously offer enormous advantages. Visiting speakers can also contribute a lot to this kind of exercise – a new face is a stimulus in itself – although care must be taken in choosing visitors, since some can have the opposite effect to that intended. It is particularly useful to consider what parents might be able to offer in this kind of situation, since among them will be experts of all kinds whose knowledge can be tapped – without fee – and this is one way of involving them in the work of their children in a more direct and mutually profitable manner than that offered by a Parent Teacher Association. A programme can be devised for one lesson or several, using devices of this kind to show pupils as many aspects as possible of the theme or area of work the teacher is about to take them into in a way that it is hoped will arouse their interest and make them want to explore further.

A second method of arousing the interest of pupils, which may be applicable to some kinds of theme, is a visit or series of visits to places in the locality that have some bearing on the area of work to be explored. A visit to a local factory engaged in some industrial process that is based on the scientific principles it is hoped the pupils will come to understand, a visit to the docks to see the kind of cargo that is being handled and its origins, a 'nature walk', a visit to the local church or any kind of outing that can be devised to show pupils aspects of the project can be expected to arouse more interest than the most inspired lesson in the classroom. Nor do such visits need to be to rather obvious and special places like the local zoo or the Tower of London. A moment's thought will reveal to the imaginative teacher what he can bring to the notice of his pupils even on a walk around the vicinity of the school, if such a walk is carefully planned. Much can be done to arouse interest in certain kinds of theme by this kind of planned outing.

A third way of stimulating the interest of pupils in the work about to be undertaken is to surround them with examples of what they could do and perhaps also with the materials and equipment they might be working with. This kind of technique has proved highly successful in many infant and junior classrooms where teachers have long known the value of creating a number of displays, each related to some particular interest or activity – measuring, weighing, number, reading and so on – and allowing children to be stimulated simply by looking at these displays in passing, as it were. An exhibition is often seen by teachers as a kind of end-product of work on a theme of the kind we are describing, but many of them, when they have got there, have discovered that for the pupils, rather than being a goal, the exhibition is a new starting-point. A display or exhibition can be a good way of beginning a project and a source of great stimulation for the pupils. Similarly, to be shown the materials available can also have this effect. Again, infant and junior teachers have long recognized this and known the advantages of making available to children sand trays, water containers, Cuisenaire rods and the like and allowing them to handle such apparatus informally, to 'play' with it. One can imagine secondary pupils being equally excited if, on entering a science laboratory, they found the apparatus, equipment and materials laid out and were allowed to browse among it for a while. To surround pupils by visual and other examples of what one has in store for them may be, therefore, as good a way as any of arousing their enthusiasm.

One final point needs to be made on this. Teachers should not be above manipulating such approaches to suit their own ends and purposes. Whichever method is chosen, it is worth remembering that there are advantages in stressing the less obvious aspects of the theme, since the pupils themselves will immediately see the more obvious ones, and in stressing those that for one reason or another, personal competence or educational objectives, the teacher wishes to promote. It is at this point, at the very outset, that we begin to make use of the interests of our pupils to achieve our goals.

If we have been successful in presenting the project to our pupils in a stimulating way and arousing their interest, the result of our efforts will be a class of pupils, eager, or at least willing, to get to work. Our next problem is the sheer organizational problem of getting them started on their individual or group assignments. As far as possible, this should have been planned well in advance. No matter how great the interest we have aroused, it cannot be maintained for long unless we are ready to follow it up by providing pupils with the wherewithal to begin their work. If we are engaged in the kind of project where the syllabus has been preplanned, then it is a matter merely of good classroom organization and of having clear instructions, perhaps in the form of work-cards, and the necessary materials ready to be able to get them all down to work very quickly. The same is true if we are adopting a 'circus' approach. We may be prepared to allow them some freedom in choosing where they will begin or which group they will work with, but there is nothing really complex about getting this kind of thing off the ground.

Once again it is in the freer situation that the problems are most acute. If we are really prepared to consider suggestions from the pupils, this can be a very lengthy business and without careful organization can result in chaos. It must never be assumed that because the pupils are to be allowed to make their own choices the teacher must not preplan. Without very careful and extensive preplanning disaster will surely ensue. It is not difficult for teachers to foresee most of the lines of enquiry that children are likely to come up with and, as we have said, the initial programme should have been framed to promote interest in the kind of thing the teacher is prepared for. Therefore many pupils can start work right away, even in this free kind of atmosphere. Again work-cards may be useful in providing initial guidance and the teacher must see that the resources and materials needed are ready to hand. If most can be started off in this way, the teacher is free to deal with the other cases; those with suggestions that were not foreseen and which will need careful thought and evaluation and the inevitable group of pupils who are not stimulated, inspired or even mildly interested and will need to be privately and individually stimulated or, in the last extreme, directed into something, if they are not to constitute a disruptive influence on the work of others.

From this point on, the teacher's job is to keep a careful watch on the progress of each pupil and each group of pupils. He must make sure that his pupils are really working and getting full educational value from what they are doing, that they are working with understanding and not 'going through the motions' without thinking about what they are doing. He must ensure that as far as is possible they have the materials and resources they need; he must see to it that the initial impetus of interest is maintained as long as is possible and added impetus provided as and when it seems necessary for individuals or for the whole class; he must be on the look-out for opportunities to extend the range of their work by leading them on from the point where they started to further developments that, left to themselves, they would not have contemplated or to turn them in the direction of something new if they appear to have exhausted the vein on which they started; and all the time he must be doing this against the background of the objectives he began with, modified perhaps in the light of his continuing experience of what has turned out in practice and always with consideration for the individuality of each pupil. All of this is, or should be, part of his professional skill as a teacher and can be left to that.

However, there are certain general points that he needs to keep in mind as he guides his pupils' work in this way. To begin with, he must not lose sight of the danger, already referred to, that this kind of approach can lead to undirected and haphazard learning and can degenerate into activities that have no real educational value. At the same time, his own role can be reduced to that of a store-keeper providing materials for pupils to use but no guidance as to how they should use them to further their education. It should not be the intention to set up a kind of hobbies club in which pupils do what they want and teachers provide them with the materials they need and help out with the difficult bits. This is not the object of the exercise at all. The teacher should be doing as much, if not more, teaching in this kind of situation as he does in a more formal lesson and the pupils should be working as hard, if not harder, since they should be engaged on tasks which stretch them and which make more demands than anything which they would choose to do at home as a pastime. This approach is, after all, a method of teaching not an alternative to teaching. I well remember seeing an exercise of this kind in which one particular boy was engaged in some work on cars. He was making a folder or scrapbook containing pictures of different makes of car and listing the specifications of each. The teacher – in this case a student – was standing at the front of the class handing out paper, scissors, glue and so on in whatever quantities were needed – so enthusiastically, in fact, that there was later a stationery crisis in the school. It was clear that the boy had no understanding of the figures he was listing (for example what 'cc' means and what it signifies in relation to a car's performance), and that the teacher was making no attempt to take that boy nor any other from the interest he had shown towards something more demanding. Except for the free paper and other materials, the boy was doing no more than he could have done at home. It is not for this purpose that public money is spent on sending pupils to school and training teachers to educate them.

A second danger of this kind of approach is that it can easily lead to a concentration on fact-finding exercises to the detriment of other activities perhaps of a more creative kind, that are equally important elements in education. It is easier to view enquiry, 'finding out', as something that results in the acquisition of a lot of propositional knowledge than to see that there can be other methods of exploring the world about us – through art, craft, dance or drama for example – that may not result in propositional knowledge but can certainly bring understanding of a different kind which is just as important. Indeed, this is a criticism not only of this new kind of approach to teaching, but perhaps even more of the traditional English secondary curriculum which has placed great emphasis on the 'factual' subjects but often seen little value in engaging pupils in any kind of creative activity. This has resulted in a very one-sided kind of upbringing for many children and for this the theorists must bear as much responsibility as the curriculum planners themselves. Interest-based, enquiry-based teaching, however, offers real opportunities for creative work of all kinds – creative writing, art, model-making, dance, drama and so on – but it is easy to lose sight of this fact and to allow scope only for the 'factual' subjects. There is no theme that does not have this kind of dimension to it if teachers are aware of the need to look for it. A theme on 'Women in Society', for example, undertaken with classes of secondary girls by a group of students on a teaching practice, led not only to a sociological and historical examination of the topic but also to a visit to the National Portrait Gallery to see how women have been portrayed by artists which had direct results in the creative work of some of the pupils. Even a theme as apparently 'down to earth' as 'South Yorkshire and its People', undertaken by a member of staff at Conisbrough Northcliffe County High School, was approached in such a way as to encourage the production of a good deal of creative writing alongside the geographical and sociological.[4] The teacher who is aware of the danger of allowing such projects to develop into fact-finding exercises and of the need to promote other kinds of activity must work specifically for this, and lead pupils into it by means of what he presents to them, what he encourages them to follow up and the emphases he gives to the work. In using this approach with teachers in training, we quickly became aware that the educational diet of a potential teacher has normally been such that when asked to do a piece of work he reaches for a file and starts to collect 'facts'. On one occasion, therefore, we expressly forbade such activities and insisted on a non-verbal presentation of their findings. The results were most interesting and there is no doubt that we achieved our objective, which was to show them that there is as much educational value to be gained from that kind of activity as from most of the things that traditionally go on in schools and colleges.

Finally, a word must be said about the difficulties teachers of certain subjects might have in trying to adopt this sort of approach. So far, it has been assumed that the subject involved is not a significant factor, but there are many who feel that the nature of some subjects is such as to preclude the possibility of approaching them in the ways outlined. For example, it is said that certain subjects require a 'linear' approach, that certain kinds of knowledge must be developed step by step and cannot be tackled by starting from whatever point happens to offer a link with some interest the individual might happen to have. In particular, this kind of assertion is made about the teaching of foreign languages, mathematics and science and many teachers who specialize in these subjects will claim that any attempt to approach the teaching of their subjects via individual assignments would be sure to lead to disaster. On the other hand, there are teachers of these subjects who have welcomed a change to mixed-ability groups, have happily given up relying solely on class teaching techniques and would claim no losses and some positive gains from their achievements as a result.[5]

What is the truth of the case? Once again, it would seem that we must look more closely into each situation. To some extent, the disagreement arises more from differences of objective than from different evaluations of the effectiveness of this method. Differences of objective will lead to different emphases within the teaching of a subject and it will be clear after a moment's reflection that while it may be true that some aspects of the teaching of these subjects, such as the teaching of basic French grammar, may require a linear approach, other aspects, such as the development of an awareness of the history, culture, economy and so on of the French nation, can be dealt with, and perhaps should be dealt with, by the

4 For a discussion of this project and examples of the work of one pupil involved in it, see M. Barrs, A. Hedge and M. Lightfoot, 'Language in projects', in *English in Education*, vol. 5, no. 2, summer 1971.

5 See, for example, M. Hardie, op. cit., articles 12–17.

kind of interest-based, enquiry-based methods we have been discussing. Furthermore, even the teaching of the basic 'facts' or skills may in some cases be better done by means of the individual assignment, as in the case of some of the Nuffield science projects already referred to, although here of course the aim will be not to encourage enquiry into an area of the pupil's own choice but to require each pupil to tackle a 'circus' of activities within a prescribed area or to acquire some basic skill.

Many teachers have also discovered that a linear approach even with streamed classes requires a great deal of individual help and that in the end the individual assignment is necessary here too. This was certainly my own experience when I was teaching mathematics some years ago to a third-year 'B' stream class of more than forty boys in a secondary-modern school. The range of abilities was so great – some boys able to cope with elementary algebra, others having difficulties with the most basic calculations – that individual assignments were the only way of ensuring some value for all pupils and of retaining my own sanity.

The mixed-ability class clearly creates particular problems for the subject teacher. Indeed, it is true to say that the subject teacher who is given a mixed-ability class but is required to cover a detailed syllabus with that class has been put into a paradoxical situation and presented with a problem for which there is no answer. He can accept the paradox and achieve a partial solution by streaming within the class, by dividing the class into sub-groups based on ability and taking each group through the syllabus at the pace that seems most suited to it. The subject teacher who has a syllabus that gives him more freedom of manoeuvre, however, can use the techniques we have discussed here. He can select a theme within his subject area, as we have seen – 'Mass', 'Norman England', 'Africa', 'Reptiles' or whatever – and allow for individual or group working, working from interests within that theme either by a 'circus' approach or by some arrangement for the sharing of individual findings. As always, what is needed here is some clear thinking about what one is planning to do, what one hopes to achieve by it and what seems to be the best and most effective method to adopt. For some areas of most subjects a class lesson will be necessary, but to restrict oneself to this single device for all purposes is to reject the opportunities that other approaches can bring and to limit one's repertoire perhaps rather more than is good either for the pupils or for the teacher himself.

It may be felt necessary, however, in all subjects, particularly those where it is claimed that a linear approach is crucial or those where the teacher is more at home working in a more formal way, to arrange for some straight teaching of a subject to be undertaken. Certain basic skills may well need to be provided for in this way. If this is to happen, the timetable must allow for it at set times in the week. We shall see in discussing the teaching of slow learners in the mixed-ability class that there is a need to provide special 'remedial' periods for them and for all pupils. A similar need may exist to provide periods for the linear teaching of certain subjects or for the work of certain teachers, and this can be met in the same way. All groupings within the school, including the class groupings, must be flexible enough to allow for the different kinds of provision that will need to be made to cater for individual pupils and individual teachers.[6]

In all that has been said so far we have had in mind the individual teacher working out his own personal salvation on his own class or classes and even within his own subject area. In short, we have been concerned to offer advice that any teacher could see as applicable to his own situation. It will be clear, however, from what has been said that many of these developments are likely to be easier to implement or more effective in practice if certain changes are made in the organizational structure of the school. In particular, blocks of time rather longer than the single period are needed to allow for the kind of absorption in a piece of work that this approach is designed to encourage, and collaboration between teachers of different subjects can add another dimension to this kind of teaching and, indeed, protect individual teachers from having to meet the varied demands on their knowledge that we have suggested some themes may generate. Many schools have, therefore, altered their timetables to provide blocks of time for this kind of activity and sometimes also to allow for team-teaching. Sometimes this has been done in conjunction with a change to a mixed-ability pattern of organization, sometimes in place of such a change, since, as we shall see, team-teaching can offer mixed-ability situations even in a streamed school. We must now turn, therefore, to a consideration of developments of this rather more extensive kind.

6 For a full discussion of this type of organization of the curriculum in the secondary school see Charity James, *Young Lives at Stake* (Collins, 1968), chapter 6.

Chapter 3

Team-teaching

In the previous chapter, an attempt was made to indicate some of the ways in which the individual teacher can alter his own approach to teaching towards the more individualistic methods that seem necessary to the teaching of a mixed-ability class. It was shown that a great deal can be done by the individual teacher and that the adoption of a mixed-ability form of organization does not necessarily entail a move to some form of team-teaching. Conversely, it is also the case that team-teaching can be undertaken in a streamed school and the streamed divisions can be maintained within it. In short, mixed-ability groups do not require team-teaching nor does team-teaching require mixed-ability groups. However, in practice the two are often found together. In particular, team-teaching is usually found in schools where there has been a change to mixed-ability groups and is sometimes used as a means of effecting such a change, since it is possible to introduce some mixed-ability working through a team-teaching programme even within a school whose basic organizational structure is a streamed one. No discussion of mixed-ability teaching would be complete, therefore, without a full examination of the practicalities of team-teaching.[1]

There is little doubt that team-teaching, properly organized, planned and executed, can give an added dimension to the kind of teaching we discussed in chapter 2 (nor that, if not properly organized, it offers more scope for chaos than most teaching methods). A general aim of this kind of approach to teaching is variety and flexibility and team-teaching can increase both. There is more scope for working through pupils' interests, since we no longer have to decide either to limit their range to the area of competence of one teacher or to expect that teacher to extend his area of competence to the point where in becoming wide it will also become dangerously thin, where he may become a jack of all trades and master of none. A team of teachers will bring many areas of competence and expertise into play and no member of it need surrender or compromise his specialisms. Indeed, he may in this situation be able for the first time to make full use of skills and knowledge that previously he had little or no scope for, since an interest-based approach, as we have seen, may allow for new developments in content beyond the traditional school subjects. A pupil may wish, for example, to undertake some filming or still photography and this may be seen in its context as a valuable thing for him to do, in which case a teacher who has some skill and experience in this field would be a great asset and would find a new dimension to his work. The

1 See also J. Freeman, *Team Teaching in Britain* (Ward Lock, 1969), K. Lovell, *Team Teaching* (University of Leeds, 1967) and D. Warwick, *Team Teaching* (University of London, 1971).

kind of individual assignment discussed in chapter 1, therefore, becomes easier to provide for because of the range of knowledge and expertise that a team of teachers can bring to bear on it.

Team-teaching can also provide a useful flexibility of groupings, since with a number of teachers available, pupils can be divided into groups of varying sizes according to the needs of any situation. Sometimes much time and energy can be saved by taking the whole group together for a presentation, lecture, visiting speaker or other such event that is felt to be appropriate and valuable for all; at other times, divisions can be made into groups of normal class size or into smaller groups of, say, four or five pupils for tutorial or other purposes, again according to need.

In chapter 2 stress was laid on the importance of the right kind of initial presentation to pupils. Without the motivation that this is designed to generate, little can be achieved. The same is also true of any later occasion when it is felt desirable to have some kind of presentation to all of the pupils together, either by a member of the team or a visitor. This kind of situation is more prone than any other to misfire, to promote boredom rather than enthusiasm, to end in chaos rather than purposive activity; the existence of a team of teachers, some of whom will be better at this kind of thing than others, is again a safeguard against disaster. There can be variety of contribution bringing a greater likelihood of success and less danger of failure.

A final point that must be made in listing some of the advantages of team-teaching is the fact that it gives teachers greater opportunities for discussing their work with each other. Indeed, one might go further and stress that it actually requires of teachers that they discuss their work with their fellow team members. Too often there is not enough dialogue between teachers. The individual teacher in his classroom is like a goldfish in a bowl, cut off from others and from the world outside. Some informal discussion often does go on in the common room, but there is nothing like a common task for generating real discussion between people. A team-teaching assignment makes it impossible for teachers to avoid constant and rigorous debate and reappraisal of the goals of their teaching, the content of their work and the methods that will best enable them to achieve their objectives. Some would even claim that team-teaching leads to better preparation of work, since the work of each individual is open to the scrutiny of his colleagues and inadequate preparation lets the team down as much as the individual himself. Again, team-teaching is not, or should not be, essential for constant and rigorous consideration by a teacher of his professional concerns nor for adequate preparation of his work, but there is no doubt that it provides additional incentives to both.

Team-teaching, then, requires the collaboration of two or more teachers on a common educational purpose. This is the one common denominator of all team-teaching situations. Beyond this there is quite rightly infinite variety. Teams vary considerably in size. Logically, of course, they cannot contain fewer than two teacher members; seldom do they contain more than eight, although there is no reason, other than perhaps certain administrative considerations, why they should not. Clearly, the size of the team will depend on several factors, but the key factor must always be the number of pupils that is being catered for. It would be unrealistic to plan for a teacher–pupil ratio that was very much better than that allowed for in the overall staffing of the school. One teacher for each class of pupils involved in the exercise, therefore, would seem to be the general rule. If an extra member can be made available, then this is all to the good.

Similar variation can be found in the sizes of pupil groups. Some schools have undertaken team-teaching with single classes, although obviously such generous staffing has to be paid for elsewhere in the timetable. At the other extreme, there are occasionally team-teaching programmes that involve the whole school. However, such work is most commonly undertaken with year groups, divided into two if they are particularly large, so that the optimum size for most purposes would seem to be three or four classes, 90–120 pupils. It is also most usual to find this kind of approach being used with the first and second years in the secondary school, although many have found it valuable in the final year, particularly with leavers and other pupils not preparing for public examinations, when these are being taught separately from their colleagues, and some schools have seen it as an essential element in the teaching of every year throughout the school. It is also increasingly common to see forms of team-teaching in primary schools.

There is no one answer to the question of how much time should be allocated to this kind of work, since almost every variation can be observed. As so often is the case, it is a matter of adapting to local conditions. Some certainly would be prepared to devote all of the working week to a team-teaching project, but it does seem important to remember, as we saw in chapter 2, that many things that might be regarded as vital cannot be dealt with in such a programme – the basic skills of reading, number and learning a foreign language, for example, and remedial work of all kinds – so that it is probably safer to see this as only one aspect of a total curriculum not as a curriculum in itself. Furthermore, it is always possible to have too much of a good thing and it is difficult for any of us to sustain an interest, however absorbing, from Monday to Friday unrelieved. Most schools, therefore, allocate only a part of the week to work of this kind. Some have followed the primary pattern of allotting it every afternoon; others have given it a day like the primary 'integrated day'; yet others have found three or four half-days per week for it. In practice it is a matter of extracting what time is possible in the face of the many other competing interests and the general consensus seems to be that three half-days per week, ten to twelve periods, is quite adequate and possibly sufficient for most undertakings of this kind.

The last important variable is the range of work that a team-teaching programme is to cover. Team-teaching is used both in situations where a very detailed syllabus has been drawn up and in situations where an enquiry-based, interest-based approach is being used. It is used within particular curriculum subjects and where there are no restrictions as to subject; sometimes in fact it has been used to break down subject barriers. Most often it is associated with a move towards some form of 'integrated studies', although not always with a change to an enquiry-based approach. In practice, the range that a team-teaching project is designed to cover will again depend on local factors, on the proportion of the working week devoted to it, on the subjects that have 'given up' their share of the time-table to allow it to be introduced and on the departments and individuals who are interested in this development and willing to be associated with it. Such local factors most often mean that it becomes a humanities project – there may be a parallel, but separate, team-teaching project in the sciences or they may continue to be taught in a traditional manner. Occasionally, it will be possible for it to cover a full range of subjects. The latter is probably the ideal situation, especially if it is felt desirable to allow the pupils as much freedom of enquiry and exploration as possible, but the important thing is to be clear in advance about the particular situation that prevails, about what should be done and about what can and cannot be done. Any kind of team can work, provided that its members know where they are going, what they can cope with and what they must leave to some-one else.

Infinite variety is possible in the type of work undertaken by a team and the type of team that might be developed to deal with it. Whatever kind of team we eventually go for, however, its work can be made or marred by the kind of administrative arrangements made for it. Team-teaching makes greater and more complex demands on the expertise of teachers than class teaching of a traditional kind and we are inviting disaster and being hardly fair to the teachers involved if we expect them to undertake this work without being given, as far as is possible, conditions to work in that, if not ensuring success, will at least not provide them with additional hurdles to surmount.

A first essential requirement and one which applies, as we saw in chapter 2, to all individual and group assignment work, whether associated with team-teaching or not, is that the timetable should allow substantial blocks of time in which the work of pupils can be developed. This kind of teaching is impossible in single periods of forty minutes or so. If the interest of the pupil is to be maintained, he must be given the opportunity to put in a decent amount of work on whatever he is engaged on each time he comes to it. He must be allowed to become absorbed in what he is doing, to see something definite for his efforts and to end each session with the knowledge that he has made observable progress. Some will not be absorbed, of course, or will finish a particular piece of work quickly. These can be moved on to something else. But the pupil who is involved must be given time to achieve something substantial and not be moved from one thing to another, like a rat or a pigeon, by a bell or a buzzer that interrupts him every forty minutes, since in these conditions it is difficult to see how any real habits of study can be developed. It is often said that children cannot concentrate for long periods of time – this has been the justification of the short school period – but we have all seen quite small children 'lost' in something that really interests them for much longer periods than that. It is this ability to become absorbed in something of genuine interest that we must try to capitalize on.

Furthermore, the teacher needs substantial blocks of time with his pupils. In a situation where he is not offering them all a short formal lesson but is concerned to work with groups or individuals engaged on different kinds of work, he needs time to get around to all of them, to see where they have reached, to advise on where they should go next, to prod those who are slacking, to make sure that the eager ones do not lose their enthusiasm through a lack of books, materials or encouragement. To ask anyone to work in this way in forty-minute bursts is to invite failure for the project and neurosis for the teacher.

On the other hand, it is equally important not to provide periods of time that are so long that interest becomes difficult to sustain. It is better, of course, to err on this side, since the teachers can always break up the time allotted and vary the programme to avoid boredom. Blocks of time roughly equivalent to three normal periods seem to be the optimum here. This is why many schools prefer to allocate whole afternoons to work of this kind rather than whole mornings which in most schools are rather longer.

Blocking time for team-teaching in this way makes the task of drawing up a timetable for the school rather easier than it is when one has to timetable single and separate periods for each subject. In the long term, therefore, it is to the administrator's advantage also to make this kind of provision. In the short term, where such an arrangement is to be superimposed on an existing timetable of a traditional kind, it can be a real headache. What one must try to do is to run together the time allotted to those subjects that have opted to 'come in' on the team-teaching programme. Another solution is to switch to double-period timetabling for all purposes, so that one is looking for blocks of two double periods rather than three or four single periods to run together for team-teaching and can in any case, if in difficulty, offer double periods by themselves, since this now gives eighty minutes rather than forty.

The other main area in which team-teaching is dependent on the efforts of the administrator is that of accommodation. The two central considerations here are that there should be a variety of rooms available, or that what rooms are available should be capable of a variety of uses, and that they should be as close to each other as possible. It has already been pointed out that one of the advantages of team-teaching is that the size of teaching units can be varied to suit all possible educational needs. This can only be done if accommodation is available to suit teaching groups of all sizes, including a room that will accommodate the whole group at once. Some new schools have purpose-built accommodation for this kind of work with large rooms that can be divided into several small rooms by partitions or that can be given a number of 'corners' where different kinds of activity can be centred. However, few schools have the advantages of flexible spaces of this kind and in practice most have to rely on the hall and several adjacent classrooms (another timetabling complication when the hall has to be used as a gymnasium and perhaps as a dining-room also). It is interesting to note that some of the older buildings with several rooms opening on to a central hall offer better accommodation for this kind of work than many of the modern palaces of glass and concrete.

Rooms need also to be of different types as well as of different sizes. Working from children's interests can generate a lot of practical activity – dance and drama, as well as graphics and model-making – and workshop facilities of all kinds are needed. Where such facilities cannot be provided on a permanent basis, it is sometimes enough to provide occasional help by allocating such accommodation for part of the time allotted to team-teaching or by arranging for the occasional pupil to work in a corner of a workshop if he has something urgent to be done – handicraft teachers are usually particularly ready and able to allow informal work of this kind. However, if no such facilities can be made available, one can do no more than discourage children who express a desire to do something that re-quires them.

The last important requirement in accommodation for team-teaching is that the rooms allocated are as close to each other as possible. No team should be expected to play at home and away at the same time. I have known situations where the rooms allocated to the team were at different ends of a large building. Not surprisingly, in such circumstances no real team-work can flourish. Movement between groups ought to be as easy as possible and there ought to be ample opportunity for teachers and pupils to see the work of the other groups as well as of their own. Without such minimal interchange, there can be little that merits the name of team-work and, while formal arrangements can be made to allow for it, there is much to be said for informal and continuous interchange. In any case administra-tion ought to make the teacher's job easier not more difficult.

Given an organizational set-up that is as supportive as it can be in the particular circumstances of the school, teachers can begin to plan their work as a team. As in chapter 2, it will be assumed that if it is the inten-tion to work through an agreed and preplanned syllabus, teachers will need no help with how to do that and attention will be concentrated on what is needed for the planning and carrying out of an interest-based, enquiry-based project. The general idea will be to present an area of work to the pupils in the most stimulating way possible and to encourage and assist individual and group enquiry within that broad area. This approach was discussed at some length in chapter 2 in relation to the work of indi-vidual teachers. We must now consider some particular points that need to be borne in mind when it is being carried out by a team of teachers.

Paradoxically, the more freedom it is intended that the pupils should have, the more detailed needs to be the preplanning and organization of the project. This is the first point that must be made clear. Many teachers feel that there can only be freedom for pupils if they go into their class-rooms without any plan or preconceived ideas, to 'see what happens', 'play it by ear', 'allow it to develop spontaneously' or with some other such intention that makes them sound more like jazz musicians going to a jam-session than responsible educators setting about their task. The best one can say about this view is that it reveals some confusion over the concept of 'freedom'. The only freedom a teacher can be concerned with is that freedom that might be found in an educational situation. To create a free educational situation requires great skill on the part of any teacher and, no matter how experienced he is, a great deal of forethought, preplanning and careful organization. This is especially necessary when it is a co-ordinated piece of team-work that is required. Nothing that can be done in advance should be left to the hurly-burly of the classroom itself, but at the same time one must not preplan that which should be left for on the spot decision and thus impose a rigidity that will deprive both teachers and pupils of the kind of freedom this approach is designed to give them.

The first point that will need to be clarified is the area of responsibility of each member of the team. Some teams will include administrative staff; in time there may be assistants or aides formally employed in secondary schools some of whom will be attached to teaching teams; some teams may already include other non-teachers invited to make some specific contribution to the work. It is assumed that the role of such members of the team will be clear. The position of the teacher-members must be made equally clear. Some, or all, may be expected to take existing forms or classes within the project or it may be the intention to regroup the pupils according to the areas of their interests – this would seem to be a more logical method of grouping – so that some or all of the teacher-members of the team may be required to take responsibility for groups of pupils working in particular areas. A team preparing for the project on 'Communi-cations' referred to in chapter 2, for example (see pp. 20–21) would clearly be well advised to plan for groupings of pupils centred on the historian, geographer, scientist, social scientist, English and expressive arts special-ists. Pairing of teachers might also be used where appropriate, two teachers being given joint responsibility for a larger group. On the other hand, it may be the intention that one or two teachers be given a roving commission – to help with the graphic presentation of the work of pupils in all the groups, for example, to guide all the practical work that is done, to attend to the audio-visual needs of all groups or to provide any service of this kind that makes it impossible or undesirable that they be limited to one group. It may be possible, of course, to arrange that both functions be fulfilled by one person. There are many possibilities here. What matters is not so much the particular *form* of organization that is chosen as that each member should be clear about it and about his own responsibilities within it and that at any one time every pupil should know which teacher is immediately responsible for his work.

It is also very important that the method of decision-making is clearly specified and this raises the question of the leadership of the team. In many schools, leaders of teams have been appointed by the head teacher; in some cases such appointments have been formalized by the award of some kind of responsibility allowance. There are difficulties in this kind of arrangement. In the first place, it has often worked out that such a leader, while responsible for the work of the team, has not been himself an active member of it, since his administrative responsibilities elsewhere in the school have made it impossible for him to involve himself fully, or at all, in the team's project. Clearly, decisions should not be made by someone who, no matter how competent and experienced a teacher, has not an intimate knowledge of what is going on. However, even when such an appointed leader is an active and full-time member of the team, there are difficulties in the notion of collaborative team-teaching in a situation where the team is to work under the direction, however benign, of an appointed leader. On the other hand, similar, if not more serious, problems arise if one allows a leader to emerge from the membership or to be elected from it. Such a person can be more dominating and restrictive of the freedom of other members of the team, albeit through charm, personality and ability rather than official status, than any appointed coordinator. On the whole, it would seem better to maintain the democratic ethos of the team-teaching approach to education by adopting some form of rotating chairmanship, allowing decisions to be taken in an entirely democratic manner and requiring each member of the team to take his turn as chairman having executive responsibility only and being a general factotum and dog's-body for about a week at a time.

Sometimes a team project may be based on a 'core' subject, or a 'core' subject may appear as the work proceeds. In this kind of situation the teacher responsible for that subject will inevitably play a leading role in planning and carrying out the project. Where a 'natural' leader of this kind emerges, there is little point in depriving him of the opportunity to guide the work of the team, since he is best qualified to do so. Furthermore, it sometimes happens that different subjects and specialisms come to the fore at different stages in the development of the work. To allow the teachers associated with these subjects to take on the leadership of the team when their own specialism is in the ascendant is to allow a kind of natural rotation that would seem to offer the best of both worlds. Again, however, the really important thing is that the method of arriving at decisions should be clear to all from the outset.

This is, of course, one aspect of the larger problem of the extent to which teachers should be able to participate in the making of decisions within the school. The arguments just offered would seem to have a similar application here, since, as we said earlier, organizational and other changes will only work if teachers accept them and believe in them and teachers can only work successfully in the way we are suggesting if they have some genuine say in the organization of their work. If team-teaching implies collaboration, as it must, then this must be taken to its logical conclusion as one aspect of a wider pattern of collaboration within the school.

Once the team has been given a definite structure in this way, attention must be turned to planning for the work that is to be undertaken with the pupils. In the first place, a clear view of the objectives of the project should be reached by discussion, which it is hoped will end in some kind of mutual agreement. Then attention must be turned to method. There are two aspects of this. First, as much detailed preparation as possible needs to be made for the activities that pupils are likely to be engaged in and the subject-matter they are likely to need to have presented to them in one form or another.[2] Secondly, careful planning is necessary of an organizational structure that will ensure the continued smooth running of the exercise.

Preparation of material for pupil enquiries and other forms of pupil activity can be broken down into the three areas discussed in chapter 2 – selection of a theme, planning an 'impact' session or some other form of initial presentation and preparing for the demands that will be made by the pupils if an impact is achieved. Much the same considerations apply when this approach is adopted by a team as when it is undertaken by an individual. The theme should be chosen and its presentation planned with due regard for the interests and the areas of competence of all members of the team, such interests and areas of competence being thought of in wider terms than subject specialisms. As was mentioned before, those areas should be emphasized that are less likely to occur naturally to the pupils themselves, those aspects of the theme that the overall objectives of the project or general educational considerations would indicate need to be emphasized and those areas that it is felt might be less popular. As we said before, it is here that manipulation of pupils' interests starts. One must have due regard for organization and avoid the embarrassment of finding three-quarters of the group choosing one area, with the rest divided among the other three or four areas prepared for. Some balance is necessary and we must work for it from the beginning. If we are promoting a study of the local environment, for example, we can take it for granted that some pupils will want to undertake a traffic census, or explore the history of the local football team or unravel the mysteries of the local bus service without any stimulation from us. Few will immediately think of looking into the pollution problems of local industry, the leisure problems of local youth or the cultural opportunities the neighbourhood does or does not offer. Yet these may be the very areas of enquiry our team is most competent to help with and they may be felt to be of more educational value to the pupils than those they naturally come to themselves. These,

2 For detailed examples of this kind of planning of integrated studies projects, see the work of the Keele Integrated Studies Project in *Schools Council Integrated Studies: An Introduction to Integrated Studies* and *Schools Council Integrated Studies: Teachers' Guide* (Schools Council/OUP, 1972). For an account of several integrated studies schemes, see D. Warwick, *Integrated Studies in the Secondary School* (University of London, 1973).

then, would be the areas to stress in our initial presentation – by visits, films, talks from local people and so on.

We must next prepare for the fevered enquiries we are hoping to provoke. We must be able to get those who are ready down to work immediately, before their enthusiasm wears off, and to do this we must have the necessary materials and apparatus prepared and some clear indication of how they can best get started. Work-cards, provided we take care not to make them too restrictive, can be very helpful in getting groups of pupils and individuals started and we can prepare this sort of thing for as many lines of enquiry as we have been able to envisage in advance. We must also do as much work as possible ourselves in the area or areas of enquiry we are to be responsible for, since we need to be able to deal with questions that the pupils will raise, we need to be able to offer many ideas for lines of enquiry to pupils who have not been initially fired to explore anything and we need the background knowledge that will enable us to lead all pupils on from where they start to something that is worthwhile and which stretches them. All of this preparation needs to be done by the team and for the team; teachers must learn to live with a situation in which material they themselves prepare is used by others. This is what collaborative team-work implies.

No matter how thorough the preparation of material has been, little will be achieved unless equal care is taken in creating an efficient organizational structure within which the work can go on. A programme must be prepared of any further sessions that are planned with the whole group or any other large unit together. Everyone in the team must know if and when such events are to take place and everyone must be carefully briefed by those responsible for such occasions about their purposes and the ways in which they can be followed up. Very detailed arrangements must be made for the initial grouping of pupils if this is to be done on a basis other than the existing class divisions, and for their movement from one group to another if and when this becomes appropriate; when, for example, a particular line of enquiry has ended or has led on to further explorations that can best be guided by another member of the team. Arrangements should also be made for pupils to see each other's work. This is especially important where each is being allowed to explore in depth one aspect of the theme only; although there is a lot to be said for permitting informal sharing of findings, if he is to see other aspects of it, there must also be formal arrangements which will ensure that sharing does go on – regular reporting-back sessions, ongoing exhibitions or something of this kind.

Perhaps the most important area where most detailed organization is required is that of keeping an up-to-date record of the whereabouts, the assignment and the progress of each individual pupil. Unless this can be done, team-teaching will offer countless opportunities for time-wasting, repetition and even truancy. A careful record must be kept of all the children for whom each member of the team is responsible, so that none can go 'absent' without being detected. Although interchange of pupils between groups is to be encouraged, actual movement about the school during lesson time is in most cases not advisable. If it is felt that a particular pupil should be moved to another classroom, arrangements should be made between the teachers concerned in advance of the lesson so that his movement can be checked at both ends. If there has to be informal movement, it is better that it be of staff than of pupils. It is vital too that a detailed record be kept of what each pupil does, partly to ensure that he is doing something and that what he is doing represents a fair amount of work for that particular individual, and partly to see that he is not engaged yet again on the same piece of work that he did in last term's project and that of the term before that. It is only detailed organization that will protect the teacher from wastrels and enable him to ensure that all pupils get a balanced educational diet.

Finally, the winding up of an exercise of this kind needs to be carefully planned, as does a method of evaluating the extent to which the objectives proposed at the beginning have been achieved. Again, it is essential that the team plan this as a team, so that the way of drawing things to an end can be agreeable to all and the methods of evaluation such as to ensure that what each member of the team has been doing can be properly assessed. Almost certainly it will not be possible to make plans for this sort of thing before the work begins; in fact, it is most unlikely that it will be possible to do much about it until the project is well under way. This underlines the need, therefore, for continuous planning throughout the period of the project. A great deal of preplanning must be done but this will achieve little without regular and continuing opportunities for consultation, evaluation, recording and further planning. Preplanning can provide too rigid a structure; this can only be avoided if the team meets regularly to evaluate progress and make further plans in the light of experience. It cannot adequately cope with the problem of wastrels and other difficult pupils; they can only be attended to if the team meets regularly to discuss, to share experiences and to keep detailed records of what each group and each individual has done. Often this is left to informal contact of team members over coffee, lunch and so on. Too much is at stake for it to be left to casual contact of this kind. Team meetings should be formally time-tabled to take place regularly when all members of the team can attend. They should be as frequent as seems necessary, but there should never be fewer than one per week. The success of team-teaching depends on careful organization and the coordination of the efforts of all members of the team. This can only be achieved by ensuring that all planning is done formally and jointly and that each member has as full a view as possible of the general context in which he is working.

Given a structure of this kind with regular opportunities to acquire a developing understanding of the objectives and general principles of the work in hand, the individual teacher must, in the light of that understanding, guide the work of the pupils he is particularly responsible for, leading them on, passing them on to other colleagues if and when this seems the right thing to do, ensuring that all are working, that all are stretched and that all are getting value from their work. All of this can be left to his professional judgement.

We must now turn, finally, to a consideration of some of the particular problems that arise when a team-teaching approach is adopted and some of the more common pitfalls that should be avoided. All of the difficulties that we discussed in the last chapter in relation to the adoption of an assignment approach by the individual teacher will, of course, apply equally to the team-teaching situation. Undirected activity, a 'hobbies' approach, is as easy to slip into in a team context as it is when working on one's own. Similarly, it is just as easy to lose sight of the opportunities offered for creative work, except in so far as there may be a member of the team whose specialism is of this kind and who will or should make it his business to keep this objective to the forefront of things. The difficulties of certain subjects, especially those that require the learning of certain skills, also need as careful consideration by the team as we tried to show they merited from the individual teacher. All of these difficulties must be kept in mind and planned for, but all of them were fully discussed in chapter 2 and, therefore, need no further elaboration. Team-teaching, however, brings further problems of its own and these must be considered here.

In the first place, we must be aware of the host of psychological problems that arise for teachers from the kind of reorientation that team-teaching requires of them. We have already referred in passing to the need for teachers to accept that work they have prepared might be used by other members of the team. This is only one aspect of what becomes necessary when teachers move from a situation in which they have had a great deal of personal and individual freedom to one in which they must modify all aspects of their work and accept on all fronts those limitations that become necessary when several people work together. A degree of personal autonomy is lost by all members of the team in decisions concerning the objectives, content and methods of their work. Each member must to a large extent accept the objectives and the structure of the team, since unless he does so the team cannot function smoothly, it cannot work as a team and will quickly break up. A common philosophy must be developed which has, for the most part, the allegiance of all the teachers involved, since again no team can get very far if there is no agreement over goals and priorities. The development of such a common philosophy will usually entail a certain amount of compromise on the part of all the team's members and such compromise is not always easy to make.

At least two things follow from this. First, teachers must learn to gain their satisfaction from the successes of the team as a whole and not merely look to their own personal achievement. They will thus perhaps become reconciled to seeing others using material they have prepared, others operating in spheres they may perhaps have once thought were their own and others learning from them and copying their ideas. They must learn to cast their bread upon the waters, to accept sharing as a normal part of the job and to evaluate their work in terms of its total value for the pupils rather than the sense of personal achievement it gives to them.

Secondly, we must accept the fact that not all teachers may be temperamentally suited to team-teaching, not all may be able to make the psychological adjustments necessary for working in such a context. This will be especially the case with teachers who have not been prepared by their initial training for work of this kind and this may explain why many head teachers have found particular difficulties when older members of staff have been asked to involve themselves in this kind of work. On the other hand, it may be the case that what really matters is not the temperament of the individual nor his age nor the type of training and experience he has had, so much as the relative temperaments and backgrounds of all the team members. It may be that difficulties experienced when older teachers were attached to teams arose not from the fact that they were older as from the fact that they were older than other members of the team and that the spread of age and experience made it difficult to develop the community of purpose and interest that we have said is so vital. In practice, both kinds of situation will be found and both need to be guarded against. Some teachers of all ages will never be able to make the necessary adjustments to enter a team project; all teachers will only be able to do so if they can achieve a psychological 'fit' with their fellow team members. We must also guard against a situation that will inhibit or stifle the individuality of the brilliant but idiosyncratic teacher. Such a teacher has a great deal to offer if the team can adapt itself to his idiosyncracies. If a working relationship cannot be developed, however, it would be better to let him have his head in another context where collaboration is not so essential.

In addition to a reorientation to their work and the development of new attitudes towards and relationships with each other, team-teaching requires teachers to engage in a lot of rethinking of their own subject specialisms. Mention has already been made of the need for a reappraisal of the content of our teaching of a subject in order to relate it more closely to our objectives. Team-teaching necessitates a reappraisal of the content of our teaching in relation to other subjects, to other forms and fields of knowledge. As has been pointed out, team-teaching is possible within subject areas, but most team-teaching projects span a number of subjects and, although it is possible to retain subject boundaries within such a project, in practice these barriers become blurred, even if they do not disappear altogether; in fact, team-teaching is often undertaken with the specific intention of breaking them down. Furthermore, if team-teaching is also associated, as it would seem it should be, with an enquiry-based, interest-based approach to learning, it is difficult to retain such barriers; subject integration in some form will follow almost inevitably. It is not my intention here, nor would it be appropriate, to become involved in the arguments that rage over the respective merits of disciplinary and interdisciplinary teaching and learning. Nor would I wish to, since such argument has always seemed to me fundamentally misguided and to engage in it would be to reveal the same lack of subtlety and sophistication we have found reason to regret elsewhere in theoretical discussions of education. As so often, the important question is not which approach we should adopt to the exclusion of the other, but rather in what situations each is most appropriate. It is quite clear that the logic of a subject, the rigour of a discipline, can never be ignored in the teaching of it. It should be equally clear that there are many areas in which we need to develop the understanding of our pupils where an interdisciplinary approach is unavoidable. The work of the Schools Council Humanities Curriculum Project[3] has drawn attention to many areas in which integration of this kind is vital. No adequate examination of racial problems or relations between the sexes, for example, can be undertaken within any one discipline; issues of this kind must involve us in excursions into many subject areas, if we are to come to grips with them successfully. Indeed, quite often an examination of topics of this kind will take pupils into 'subjects' other than those traditionally associated with the school curriculum. It is not possible, for example, to examine the problems of relations between the sexes without considering the anthropological evidence of the pubic and marriage rites of other cultures, the law and its pronouncements on divorce, prostitution, pornography, homosexuality and abortion and the psychological factors involved in sexual relationships, in addition to the biological, sociological, historical and literary aspects of this topic that are already touched on in a traditional curriculum.

Teachers must be clear, then, about what they are contributing to a team-teaching project. There is always a danger that they will want to evaluate it in terms of how much of history or science or some other discipline each pupil is involved in. These are not necessarily the appropriate criteria to employ. If the agreed objectives of the team are to develop the ability of the pupils to think historically, to think scientifically or to acquire the essentials of some other discipline, then this is the kind of criterion to appeal to, but if the goals are other than this – to develop a greater awareness of the local environment, an appreciation of man's achievements or an understanding of human relationships – then each teacher must accept that his 'subject' will become subsidiary to the stated end. Conversely, he may find he has other 'subjects' to contribute to the combined strength of the team, interests that hitherto his work has given him no real scope for. Again it is a matter of being clear about objectives and seeing the education of the individual pupil as the goal, rather than the propagation of a particular body of subject-matter or even a particular discipline.

Finally, attention must be drawn to the fact that team-teaching does create particular problems for certain subjects. Mention was made in chapter 2 of some of the difficulties experienced by teachers of foreign languages, mathematics and science in adapting to the individual approach required by the mixed-ability group. Similar problems arise when attempts

3 See L. Stenhouse, *Journal of Curriculum Studies*, 1968, and *The Humanities Project: An Introduction* (Heinemann, 1970).

are made to involve these subjects in a team-teaching scheme and again the solution lies in careful and rigorous analysis of the objectives of the scheme. More serious, however, to my mind, are the problems that arise for art and craft specialists in a team-teaching situation. If they do not assert themselves, they can easily find themselves relegated to the role of advisers on the display and presentation of work that has been done in other subjects for other members of the team. Too often, art in a team-teaching project becomes a kind of handmaiden, concerned merely with illustration and presentation, and no really creative work is generated. This is easy to understand. For if one wants a diagram and there is an artist in the team, or if one wants a model made and the team contains a craftsman, who better to get to do the job? This is a role from which the art and craft teachers must be protected by the others and from which they must defend themselves. No teacher should be reduced to the role of teacher's aide nor should the opportunities which the presence of an art or craft teacher in a team can offer be squandered in this way. If the team is fortunate enough to contain an artist or a craftsmen, their skills should be used to contribute to the education of the pupils just as much as the skills of anyone else.

In spite of such difficulties, team-teaching offers teachers a great deal of scope for new, interesting and rewarding work. It is one way of taking advantage of some of the opportunities offered by a mixed-ability form of organization and an increasing number of schools are adopting it in association with this kind of reorganization. Whether one sets out to tackle a mixed-ability class alone or in a team, however, there are many other facets of the task that have to be considered if success is to be achieved. We must now turn to a discussion of some of the more important of these.

Chapter 4

Groups and Grouping

Groups play a large and important part in the lives of all of us. We are all members of a number of small groups – the family, the office or department, our circle of friends at the pub or club or church – and our membership of these groups is perhaps the single most important factor in our lives. Certainly it is through membership of these groups that our lives and attitudes are shaped and modified, and it is to these groups that we owe our most easily recognizable loyalty. We find it easier to see ourselves as members of small groups of this kind than of society as a whole. This is what Aristotle meant by his often misinterpreted dictum that 'man is a political animal', since he had in mind the Greek view of 'political' as referring to the life of a 'polis' or small city community. There is much anthropological and indeed zoological evidence to support this view of man's gregarious nature. Furthermore, there is a growing body of psychological evidence which suggests that the group, and especially the peer group, is particularly important at the adolescent stage of development for most young people – a fact that we can hardly doubt as we watch adolescents moving about our cities like clouds, ever changing their shape, forming and reforming, but seldom to be seen unaccompanied. Clearly, while we all draw strength from membership of groups, the adolescent seems to have most need of such strength, perhaps because for the most part he seems to be able to take it from only one source – the peer group.

This tendency towards group membership can be used as an effective teaching device. Indeed, it has been argued earlier in this book that it should be used as a teaching device and that the logic of the mixed-ability form of organization forces the teacher to think more in terms of individual and group work and less in terms of class teaching of a traditional kind. It has come to be an accepted method of working in infant schools; it is common in most sixth forms; it is a method often used nowadays on in-service courses and at top level conferences. If infants and adults both find it a congenial and successful way of working it is difficult to think of reasons that might exist for saying that it has no value in the years between.

If one accepts that group work is an important educational device and one that should be used at all levels of education, particularly with classes of mixed ability, then it becomes necessary to look carefully into the methods and rationale of grouping. In the first place, some attention needs to be given to the basic criteria upon which a teacher might subdivide a class into groups. There would seem to be at least four broad approaches the teacher could adopt, all of which one can find being practised at present.

First, there are many teachers who, faced with a mixed-ability class, will group the pupils according to their abilities; in other words, they will

solve the problems presented to them by the unstreamed school by streaming within the class. Pupils will be grouped according to their previous
achievements in the subject concerned and can then be pushed on at a rate
that is right for their level of attainment in a group with others whose
pace of working is roughly similar. It has already been suggested that this
may be the only way for the teacher who has to follow a detailed syllabus
in a given subject with a mixed-ability class to approach his task. In this
kind of situation the teacher prepares not one class lesson but four or five
group lessons, and thus covers the content of the course at a rate appropriate to each group. The advantage of such an arrangement is that it provides the teacher with relatively homogeneous groups to work with, while
avoiding some, if not all, of the social difficulties associated with streaming
on a large scale. Furthermore, it is relatively easy for such groupings to
be changed for different subjects or to allow for the different rates of progress of individual children. Thus it would be claimed that a pupil can be
working with fellow pupils of roughly equivalent ability in all subjects
where this kind of approach is felt to be relevant and can be readily moved
'up' or 'down' as his position changes in relation to the others. Only thus,
it would be argued, can we ensure that all pupils will be stretched and none
broken. This is possibly the most common form of grouping that one can
find in schools at the present moment.

On the other hand, it is claimed by some that grouping by ability within
a class suffers from all, or most, of the difficulties associated with grouping
by ability within the school. In particular, extraneous factors, such as
social and personal characteristics, enter into the teacher's judgement, and
the groupings that emerge turn out not to be based solely on ability at all.
Furthermore, the streamed grouping within the class then gives rise to the
kind of 'self-fulfilling prophecy' that has been shown to be associated with
streaming within the school,[1] and pupils begin to work at the level of the
group they find themselves in, to satisfy but never to exceed the expectations their teachers have of them. Even though such groupings appear to
be based on ability therefore, many able pupils are not stretched, since for
other reasons they have not been placed in a group whose expected level of
work makes real demands of them.

Many would want to argue further that to adopt this kind of approach
is in any case to miss the point of unstreaming and the opportunities it
offers. Such teachers would want to use something other than ability as
the basic criterion of grouping. An extreme form of this attempt to get
away from academic ability as the only essential criterion for organization
within a class would be to group pupils in an entirely random fashion – to
draw names from a hat or arbitrarily send them to different tables or
corners of the room as they come in through the door. Such an approach
would be likely to ensure mixed-ability groups within the mixed-ability
class, but could lead to some injudicious combinations, and would equally
ensure that the teacher gained none of the advantages that are to be gained

1 See B. Jackson, *Streaming: an Education System in Miniature* (CRKP, 1964), p. 63.

from other forms of grouping. It is not, therefore, to be recommended to any except confirmed addicts of Russian roulette.

The third basis one might have for grouping is a modified version of this approach, and would certainly be favoured by many teachers – the grouping of pupils according to friendship patterns within the class or, more strictly speaking, allowing pupils to group themselves according to friendship patterns. Friendship is a more important factor in school than perhaps many teachers realize. In particular, it has an important bearing on behaviour. It is unwise for teachers to ignore such friendship patterns, therefore, but whether they should go to the other extreme and use them as the only basis for grouping pupils is questionable. In the main one would want to question it on the grounds that it places the entire responsibility for grouping in the hands of the pupils themselves, and although the wishes and choices of pupils are important and highly relevant factors in such decisions, there must be some teacher direction too. Teachers must take control to ensure that the groups that are formed are the most appropriate for the purposes in hand. For here, as in all aspects of educational decision-making, it is the teacher's job to use what advantages a situation offers to further his educational aims.

A basis for compromise between pupil choice and teacher direction is offered by a fourth method of grouping, grouping by interest. This method presupposes, of course, an approach to teaching like that discussed in chapters 2 and 3, namely an interest-based, and perhaps also an enquiry-based, approach. If this is to be our approach, then it clearly makes sense that children should be grouped according to the interests they show, and they must be given time to get to know each other's interests and to group themselves accordingly. It is interesting to note the overlap here with grouping by friendship, since there is some evidence to suggest,[2] and many teachers will themselves have observed, that the interests pupils have outside the school seem to prove stronger than those developed in school and that friendship plays an important part in choice of activity and interest in any kind of project. This is in itself, of course, a reflection on the importance of friendship to which we have already referred and an argument for providing within the school opportunities for such relationships to develop. Some teacher direction is, however, also necessary. It has already been stressed more than once that teachers should use their pupils' interests to promote their education, and this process begins at the point where groups are formed. Even if interest, along with friendship, is the basis, teachers will need to make adjustments, and such adjustments should be made in the light of what is known about relationships within groups and of the purposes teachers might have in adopting group methods.

There are two main reasons why teachers will want to divide pupils into groups and, correspondingly, two main purposes that should be borne in mind when deciding on the methods by which they are to be so divided. Clearly, one purpose will be that of furthering their academic education.

2 See for example J. E. Allen, *Ideas*, no. 21, 1971.

Group work can be viewed as a methodological device for providing each child with the appropriate educational diet. Seen in this way, its main purpose will be to enable the teacher to ensure that all pupils are fully stretched and that none are asked to tackle problems that are beyond them. If this were the only purpose of group work, then it might be thought unnecessary to look beyond the first method of grouping discussed above, namely grouping by ability. However, implicit in the criticisms of this method is the notion that the furthering of the academic education and scholastic attainment of each pupil is not the sole aim of grouping. A further aim, which is embodied in the idea of grouping according to friendship and interests, is that of furthering their social education and this is the second kind of consideration that teachers must bear in mind when forming groups.

Some teachers, of course, would want to deny that social learning was their concern and would wish to assert that their only purpose is to further the academic progress of their pupils. This position would seem to be reinforced by recent moves towards establishing 'moral education' or 'social education' as separate 'subjects' on the timetable, developments which suggest that they can be left to the teacher responsible for those periods. It is doubtful, however, whether such a position is tenable. Time for looking at moral and social issues in a responsible way, under the guidance of someone skilled to supervise it, is no doubt of great value, but a part of social learning is the development of social attitudes and this comes about through real social relationships, teacher–pupil relationships no less than any others. Social attitudes are caught rather than taught, a truism stressed in the assertion of the Newsom Report that teachers can only escape from their influence over the moral and spiritual development of their pupils by closing their schools.[3] Social learning is the result of every teacher's relationship with his class and his method of organizing his work with that class. Indeed, there is evidence to suggest[4] that a teacher's ability contributes relatively little to the academic success of his pupils in comparison with the marked effect it has on other aspects of their development, including their social development. Social learning, then, is a function of the social organization of the school and of the class, so that it is the responsibility of every teacher. It should not be allowed to happen in a random fashion and consideration should always be given to the likely results of one's teaching in terms of the social learning it is likely to promote. It is a puzzling feature of present-day educational debate that those teachers who are concerned lest new methods bring a random element into children's academic learning, are often quite content to accept an even greater random element in their social and moral learning.

What kinds of social aim might one have in grouping pupils? What kinds of social learning might one want to encourage? At one level, one might merely wish to create a situation in which personal relationships

3 *Half Our Future* (HMSO, 1963), para. 160.
4 See K. M. Evans, *Sociometry and Education* (RKP, 1962), p. 105.

between pupils can develop or in which pupils can learn to make personal relationships. Mention has already been made of the importance of groups and personal relationships within groups to all of us. If this is so, then clearly teachers should do whatever they can to enable their pupils to learn to form such relationships and to get full benefit from them. Mention has also been made of the important part that friendships play in the lives of children and adolescents. Teachers should not undervalue such friendships nor should they lose sight of the opportunities such friendships present to them for fostering both the social and the academic development of their pupils. On the other hand, an important aspect of the social development of pupils is that they should learn to respect and work with whomever they are required to work with by the exigencies of a particular situation or by someone who has a wider perspective on the situation than their own. The development of personal relationships and the promotion of the pupils' ability to form such relationships must be one basic social aim of grouping children.

Many teachers, however, would want to go further than this and aim at the development of particular kinds of personal relationship. There has been much discussion in recent years of the respective merits of cooperation and competition in education. Some have argued that in a competitive society schools should encourage competition, to prepare children to take their place in that society, and have looked for support also to the motivational advantages that a competitive situation seems to offer. Others have offered the counter-argument that it is part of the job of education to change society and not merely to fit children to it, that at least teachers should not compromise their professional commitment to the moral upbringing of their pupils, whatever kind of ethos exists in society, and that an education motivated by competition is perhaps not strictly deserving of the name of education at all. It is not the intention here to become involved in this debate, nor is it necessary, since whatever side one takes in this argument, there is no denying that the change from streaming to unstreaming represents a move from a competitive to a cooperative system. It is the result of a general move towards a collaborative approach to education at all levels. In short, cooperation and collaboration are the fundamental principles of a mixed-ability class organization, so that in the context of our present discussion it must be taken as given that a further social aim of any subgrouping of a mixed-ability class will be the promotion of a cooperative and collaborative approach to work. The teacher should be trying to promote cooperation and collaboration and to discourage competition.

Therefore teachers must approach the task of grouping their pupils with both academic and social purposes in mind. Of course, these aims are distinguishable only at the conceptual level. In practice, they are closely interwoven, since it is clear that the social climate the teacher creates is a very significant factor in the academic development of his pupils and that many social relationships will develop out of work commitments jointly undertaken. Working with others, especially with one's friends, is obviously more attractive to many than the loneliness of working in isolation; it can add a new dimension to work the pupil enjoys and reduce the level of boredom when the work is routine. In fact much evidence[5] suggests that the social situations in which pupils learn are as important as their intellectual abilities in deciding their levels of academic achievement. If this is so, the social environment must be carefully structured by the teacher if he is to have the best chance of achieving his academic objectives. Conversely, many of the social relationships we are concerned to develop will grow out of the academic work undertaken by the group. It has been argued[6] that work is a group activity and that the social world of the adult is based primarily on his work activity. This provides us with another argument in favour of taking seriously the social education of pupils and again, if this is so, teachers must look to the work itself as a source of social learning. In practice, then, the academic and social objectives will be inextricably interwoven and to concentrate on one to the detriment of the other will be to risk missing out on both.

To take full advantage of what can be achieved through grouping techniques in both of these spheres requires a knowledge of the ways in which groups form, some of their characteristics and the kind of interaction that takes place between individuals within them. We must now turn, therefore, to a consideration of some of the factors that teachers should bear in mind when supervising the forming of groups within their classes.

Quite a lot is known about the ways in which children and young people will group themselves when given the opportunity to do so and the teacher needs to be familiar with these basic trends so that he can avoid the problems that will arise if he goes against them, and can take advantage of the opportunities that accrue if he understands and uses them.[7] To begin with, we have already referred several times to the effect of friendship patterns and out-of-school relationships and interests on the grouping of children in schools. Pupils, if given a free choice, will tend to choose to work with those with whom they have some contact outside the school, those who live near them, went to the same primary school or meet them at Church, Sunday school, Scouts, Guides or the Youth club. This tendency is completely natural. We do it ourselves. When entering a situation for the first time we look around for people with whom we have had previous associations in other contexts. A glance at the groupings which form at any PTA dance, for example, will quickly reveal to us the truth of this. We should also note that these tendencies will vary in form with the ages of the pupils concerned and that the stage of development will be a significant

5 See, for example, R. P. Amaria and G. O. M. Leith, *Educational Research*, 1969.

6 J. A. C. Brown, *The Social Psychology of Industry* (Penguin, 1954), p. 85. See also M. Hardie (ed.), *At Classroom Level* (PSW Educational, 1971), p. 77.

7 For a full discussion of these and related points, see K. M. Evans, op. cit., and D. H. Hargreaves, *Interpersonal Relations and Education* (RKP, 1972).

factor in the formation of groups. In the pre-adolescent stage, for example, boys and girls are unlikely to mix but will naturally group themselves separately. We have already referred to the advantages that can accrue when pupils are able to work with their friends in social environments they have largely been able to create for themselves. They seem to get on better, faster and with less stress, so that there are fewer behaviour problems to distract the teacher from his main task. On the whole, then, there seems to be much in favour of going along with this general tendency and allowing these friendship patterns to determine largely the composition of the working groups within the class. There are, however, some pitfalls to be avoided here which draw our attention again to the need for the teacher to exercise some control over the forming of groups.

In the first place, this tendency to maintain out-of-school relationships in groupings within the school might result in the concentration of all potential troublemakers in one or two groups. The common interest uniting such groups might be a shared desire to drive the teacher up the wall and this is not the sort of interest that provides him with scope for development into educationally profitable channels. The cement that holds such a group together may be its collective resentment of authority and this could well be the result of certain kinds of out-of-school association. After all, what distinguishes a group from a gang is no more than the different view taken of the purposes of each by society as a whole. Keir Hardie led a group; Al Capone a gang. In both cases they were at the head of small bodies of people united by a common interest and certain shared goals. In dividing his class into groups, the teacher must, therefore, avoid creating gangs or allowing such to develop.

It may well be the case, of course (indeed, one would hope that it would be) that this new approach to teaching will remove some of the causes of troublemaking and harness the energies of such pupils to more positive and constructive activities. Some will perhaps always remain and in the teacher's own interests, in those of the class as a whole and, not least, to the ultimate advantage of the troublemakers themselves, he must distribute these pupils widely and judiciously among the other groups which are forming. In doing so, he must remember that it is not enough merely to place such pupils physically at the same table or in the same corner as the group he wishes them to work with. To be successful a group must have real cohesion; all members must feel themselves a part of it and must be accepted by their colleagues as a part of it. In all cases where the teacher is adding members to groups, therefore, he must be aware of the need to show all concerned that there is a positive purpose in the change he is making, to show the group that the new member will have something of value to offer it and to show the new member that he has a role to play and a contribution to make to the collaborative enterprise. It will be an advantage if any adjustments of this kind can be made at a very early stage, since once a group has formed and begun to develop a sense of unity and group identity, it is very difficult for a newcomer to break into it.

A second danger that is endemic in giving a class complete freedom to subdivide itself is that there may well be a tendency for groupings to be based more on relative ability than the teacher may feel is desirable. Community of interests may well mean similarity of intellectual capacity, as might family or neighbourhood relationships or involvement in and attendance at the same out-of-school activities. If the teacher is aware of the importance of the social learning he is trying to promote, he will want to avoid this kind of development on any large scale and will want to ensure some kind of 'mix'. Normally, in the nature of things, this problem will resolve itself into a matter of attaching the less able, the slow learners, the non-readers to groups. Again, as in all cases where he is adding individuals to existing groupings, he will need to show all concerned that there is a valuable contribution to be made by such pupils. More will be said in a later chapter about the problems of the slow learners in the mixed-ability class. It will be enough if one merely says here that they should not be allowed to group themselves together and struggle along on some activity or project that can be seen by them and all others to be inferior. This cannot result in the learning, social or academic, that the teacher would want for any of his pupils, nor should they be separately grouped to have 'remedial work', while the others are pursuing their enquiries and their interests. It should not be difficult for a teacher to discover some distinctive contribution that such pupils can make to a collaborative undertaking. I have myself taught non-readers whose skill with paint and crayons and general ability as illustrators were far greater than my own. If social learning is to take place, we must show all pupils that educational enterprises do not always involve the skills of reading and writing, that other kinds of activity can be just as valuable, in some contexts more valuable, and that we do value these things. So much that is wrong with present-day education, especially that of the adolescent, springs from the tendency to disvalue the skills and interests of young people and create a gap between their values and those of the system. The mixed-ability class must be seen and seized as an opportunity to bridge that gap.

The third main concern of the teacher as he supervises the formation of groups within his mixed-ability class must be the situation of the isolate, the pupil who, for whatever reason, has no friends and is not generally acceptable to the existing groups. Such a pupil will, like all others, have his own interests, will choose a group to work with and has an entitlement to be allowed to work with it. The teacher's task here is particularly difficult. Not only must he be able to show a group that the new member he is offering it or who wishes to join it has a valid contribution to make to its work, he must also overcome the objections to working with this pupil as a person that other pupils will raise in the light of their previous knowledge of his unattractiveness. Furthermore, the teacher has in this situation a remedial task to perform with the individual concerned, for such a pupil is clearly backward in his skill at making personal relationships and part of the teacher's job in getting him involved in a group is to give him the help he needs in making friends and developing relationships with others. The teacher will want to avoid, therefore, the situation in which he takes such a pupil along to a group to be met by a chorus of voices loudly declaring their unwillingness to be lumbered, particularly as the unfortunate pupil concerned may have already had this experience before taking his problem to the teacher. In this kind of situation, it is especially important to move in before groups have become too fixed or have achieved too strong a sense of group identity. The teacher needs to know in advance, therefore, who the isolates are and which pupils will need particular attention from him in the early stages of group formation. He would also be well advised to keep all groups in a reasonably loose and fluid state until all of the adjustments he feels are needed have been made.

In concerning himself with this difficult problem of the isolates however, the teacher must avoid confusing them with the solitary workers. There are pupils who choose to work alone for reasons other than an inability to make relationships or to work with others. They may not choose to work alone on all occasions, but sometimes they like to. In some cases this is because of a feeling some pupils seem to have that less work is done in a group project, that they will 'get on' less well and that to ensure progress they should work by themselves. It is difficult to generalize about such pupils. Certainly one would be reluctant to force them into group work and forbid them to work by themselves. Indeed, it may be important that some pupils should learn to work alone, since many jobs require this, not least those involving study. On the other hand, it is clear that when they do work alone there can be little gain in their social education and if one of our objectives in adopting group-work techniques is to assist the development of their abilities to work with others then we must be aware that we are not succeeding in this with the solitary worker. The answer here would seem to be to allow individual working, since one does not want to cut too violently across what may be a well-developed learning style, but to keep a close watch on and careful record of those pupils who take advantage of it. It is really only those few who always choose to work alone that the teacher need concern himself with. Something can be done too by encouraging all such pupils to join in with others for occasional short-term and subsidiary projects. Flexibility of groupings is important here as elsewhere.

This question of individual and group working raises the general issue of the otimum size of groups. In addition to the solitary worker, the teacher will observe also the phenomenon of pairs. This kind of paired grouping is a feature of certain age-groups and seems to be more common among girls than among boys. Again it is something for the teacher to keep an eye on rather than to get anxious about and again it can best be dealt with if the groupings are flexible and if for some purposes such pairs can be integrated with others.

At the other extreme, there is the question of how large a group should be allowed to become. Clearly, the answer to this question will vary according to the purposes of the group concerned. It should be large enough to achieve its purposes but not so large as to exclude some members from making a full contribution to its work. Full participation of all members can probably be achieved if the group has four, five or six members. It is also in such small groups that social learning can best take place so that four to six would seem to be the norm to aim for. In practice, it is unlikely that the groupings will produce groups with a membership above eight. When they begin to reach that size, there is a natural tendency for them to subdivide themselves. This in itself is not a bad thing, since it creates some interaction between groups and this is difficult for the teacher to generate from the outside.

In supervising the formation of groups within his mixed-ability class, then, the teacher must keep a close watch on the progress of the trouble-makers, the slow learners and the isolates and must attend to the size of the groups that are forming. He must also bear in mind the need to match the learning styles of individuals and their personalities or at least to avoid the possibilities for clashes. Little is known at present about the effects of different personality characteristics on learning as such or on group learning, but individual personality will clearly have a great effect on the social climate within any group and the relationships existing between its individual members. Trouble for the teacher does not always arise from confirmed troublemakers; it can come about when two normally well-behaved pupils are set to work together and evident personality clashes result. Teachers need to give attention to this factor in the formation of groups.

Such clashes are especially prone to arise over the leadership of groups. A particularly strong and dominant character will tend to endeavour to assert authority over the group as a whole and two such characters in the same group could be a source of trouble. In this connection it should be noted that it is not always the most popular pupil who comes to leadership in such situations; more often it is the one who has the most ideas and is able to come up with suggestions which all can see are the best suggestions they have had for forwarding their common purposes.

However, we might also ask whether teachers should encourage the emergence of group leaders at all, since it would seem that, while it might do a lot for the pupil leader, this might be achieved at the expense of the development of qualities of self-reliance and confidence in the rest. Furthermore, it may not advance the learning of all to be in a situation where one pupil assumes control, since the others may come to feel alienated from the purposes of the group and motivation will thus be lost. Groups can be run by authoritarian, *laissez-faire* or democratic methods; in other words, they can have one person as leader, have no leadership at all or be subject only to decisions taken collectively by all members as equals. Experiments[8] have suggested that a democratic form of organization leads to greater

8 See, for example, R. K. White and R. Lippitt, *Autocracy and Democracy: an Experimental Inquiry* (Harper & Row, NY, 1960).

achievement on the part of all pupils and is to be preferred as a basis for educational advance. The same arguments apply here as we used when discussing leadership of a team of teachers. If all are to be fully involved in the work of the group, all must share in decision-making. Furthermore, a democratic organization would seem to be the only form consonant with the social objectives that we have described as endemic to the mixed-ability class. Pupil groups, like teams of teachers, should be organized by democratic methods so that all members feel fully involved in their activities and can learn to take a share of responsibility for those activities. Teachers should bear these factors in mind, therefore, and deal with situations where individuals tend to dominate the rest. To have a spokesman for the group will often be convenient administratively, but to avoid the dangers of this, some kind of rotation of responsibility would seem to be necessary.

If teachers are to be as sensitive to the subtleties of grouping as what has been said so far would seem to require that they should be, they will need a great deal of prior knowledge about all of their pupils. Teachers have been inclined to be more concerned with the intellectual capacities of their pupils and to pay less attention to the assessment of their social capacities, their sociometric status. Indeed, in a traditional class teaching situation, such knowledge is not nearly so important, so that there has hitherto been little reason for them to be conscious of the need for it. Concern with the social education of pupils and with the problems of grouping them suitably in a mixed-ability class makes such knowledge essential and we must look briefly now at some of the techniques available to the teacher for obtaining it.

Following the lead of J. L. Moreno,[9] psychologists have shown that relationships within a group can be revealed by relatively simple methods. If we ask all the pupils in a class to tell us whom they would like to sit by or work with or spend a day out with, suggesting that they give us in each case two or three names in order of preference (it is not advisable, although it might be more revealing, to ask them to tell us whom they would not like to sit by, work with or spend a day out with), we can get a pretty clear picture of the social relationships existing in the class at that point of time. This information will only be given freely and truthfully if we assure them of total confidentiality and indicate that as a result they will have a chance to sit by or work with, if not spend a day out with, the person of their choice. From this information we can determine the sociometric status of each individual. The information can be plotted on a simple chart, or sociogram, using a circle or some such mark for each pupil and arrowed lines linking the circles to indicate the direction of any attraction that exists in each case (see Figure 1). A clear picture then emerges of the sociometric status of each individual and the social relationships linking the individuals together. We begin to see who the isolates are, where mutual pairings exist, where there are triangular relationships and who the 'stars' are – those

9 J. L. Moreno, *Who Shall Survive?* (Washington, 1934).

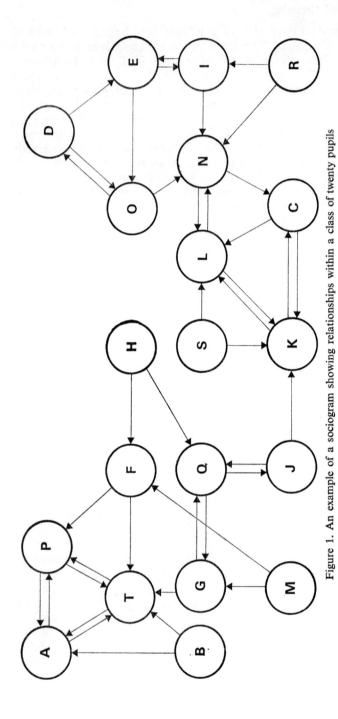

Figure 1. An example of a sociogram showing relationships within a class of twenty pupils

whose circle is surrounded by arrows pointing inwards. The same information can also be tabulated by using a graph, or sociomatrix, if the teacher finds it easier to read in this form. Pupils are listed on both axes and relationships shown in the corresponding squares like, for example, a table indicating distances between major cities (see Figures 2 and 3). Whatever form of presentation the teacher favours, however, this relatively simple test will have provided him with a great deal of the information he needs to help him with the supervision of the formation of groups.

Some words of warning must be put in here, however, before the reader rushes off to try this out. In the first place, this is only one of a number of ways in which one might set out to discover the social relationships existing in the class and it does tell us mainly about the social situation in relation to the particular question we have asked; the person a pupil wants to sit by in class may not be the one he would like to work with or to spend a day out with. Secondly, there is evidence to suggest[10] that there is a high level of stability in the sociometric status of the individual, that

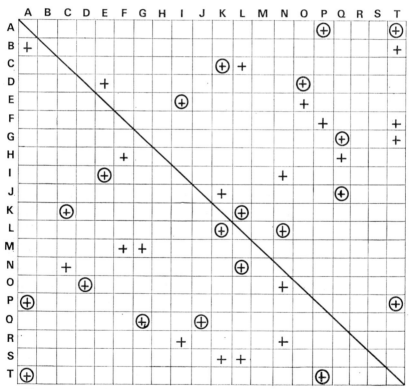

Figure 2. The same data expressed as a matrix. (+ = choice, ⊕ = mutual choice)

10 See, for example, M. L. Northway, *Educational Research*, (1968).

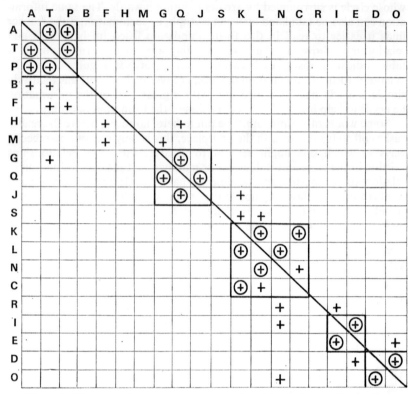

Figure 3. The same data expressed as a sociomatrix to show sub-groupings within the class

pupils who are popular continue to be popular and that isolates continue to be isolated, but, although this kind of stability exists in the individual's ability to form relationships, the pattern of relationships actually formed is changing all the time as purposes change and as the work at hand varies. In view of these factors, it is important for the teacher to remember that what he has measured is the social situation of the class at the point of time at which he asked the question and in relation to the purpose embodied in the question – sitting by, working with, going out with or whatever – and that he needs to measure the relationships within the class regularly if he is to keep abreast with developments. Such regular retesting has the added advantage that it enables the teacher at the same time to measure the success of any attempts he has been making to improve the social status of his isolates and to keep an eye on the social development of each individual. The changing nature of the relationships existing among any group of individuals is a further argument for the flexibility of grouping within the mixed-ability class which we have already advocated for a number of different reasons. It is also an argument for not being too rigid and scientific in our use of sociometric data. What we learn by using these techniques should guide but not control our decisions. It must be remembered that the basic educational criterion for grouping pupils is the area of their interests and groups must be formed with reference to those as well as to social relationships. Here again the teacher has to play several instruments at once to achieve a harmony.

The teacher who plans to group his pupils by ability in order to cover a detailed subject syllabus with them will obviously have less room for manoeuvre here and less scope for considerations of the kind we have been discussing. He is committed to the kind of emphasis on academic learning that must be at the expense of any real concern with social development. Nevertheless, he would be well advised not to ignore the social relationships that exist in his class even when grouping pupils by ability since, as we have seen, careful grouping can promote the academic learning he is seeking and contribute to the avoidance of disruptive problems of control.

Once these groups have been formed and the formation of them has been supervised along the lines that have been indicated, the teacher will need to get them going on their work by way of an organization something like that suggested in chapters 2 and 3. He will need to spend time with all of them and this creates for him the practical problem of getting round to all in the time he has at his disposal, to give them the help that we suggested was needed. He can spend a brief time with all or he can devote more sustained attention to a few each time he has the class. The latter would seem to be the better policy but it will depend on the success with which he has been able to select and organize his resources, since the other groups will only be able to get on if they have at hand the materials and other resources they need. The organization of resources is the teacher's next major problem.

Chapter 5

Resources for Teaching and Learning

The story is told of how Periander, on becoming tyrant of the Greek city of Corinth in the sixth century BC, sent a messenger to the long-established and highly successful tyrant of Miletus, Thrasybulus, to ask his advice on the mode of government he should adopt. Thrasybulus said nothing, but took the messenger out of the city and into a field of corn and, as they walked through this field, he broke off and threw away every stalk of corn that rose above the rest. As long as teaching has gone on, resources have been needed to aid and support it. That such resources have not always been successful is illustrated by the fact that when Periander asked his messenger on his return to Corinth what Thrasybulus had said, he answered that he had said nothing and Periander had to do a lot of questioning before any message came through. Not all teaching aids, however, are as deliberately obscure as this. Teachers have always been on the lookout for materials and apparatus that would help them to teach more effectively and their pupils to learn more quickly and more permanently. Most of the things they have used have been somewhat more manageable than fields of corn but there is nothing new about the use of resources for teaching and learning, other than perhaps the name.

However, interest in this problem of resources has in recent years increased considerably at all levels of educational discussion. Research in this field is being sponsored from several national sources including the Schools Council and the National Council of Educational Technology; two individual Schools Council projects, the Humanities Curriculum Project and the General Studies Project, have devoted a great deal of attention to the development of resources in connection with their own work; several Local Authorities, many individual schools and a number of Colleges of Education are building up resources centres, banks and collections; and teachers are becoming increasingly aware of the need to devote much of their attention to the development, application and storage of resource materials of all kinds.

There are two main reasons for this increase in interest. In the first place, technological developments have put a great deal more at the teacher's service and provided him with a greater variety of resource material to choose from. Traditional resources such as books, charts, pictures and so on are available to him in greater numbers and at a relatively cheaper cost than was once the case because of developments that have led to a greater facility of production. New and cheaper reprographic methods enable him to produce a wider range of materials himself. At the same time, the variety of resources available has been considerably extended by the development of new types of resource, again at a cost that makes them less of a luxury than was once the case. Such things as film-strips, audio-

and video-tapes and transparencies for use with overhead projectors are now well within the reach of the average school budget, as is the 'hardware' required to make use of them, and teachers must now choose from such a large range of sources that making the right choice on educational and economic grounds has become a problem on a scale that could not have been envisaged in the days of chalk, talk and textbooks.

The second main reason for the recent increase of interest in resources is that curriculum changes and changes of organization have presented teachers with teaching situations for which the resources they have used in the past have often proved inadequate. A mixed-ability group, for example, cannot be adequately catered for by the provision of a copy for each pupil of all the basic textbooks; each will need to be provided with the books and other resources that will meet his own individual needs. This will be true even in a situation where it is the teacher's concern to deal only with one subject area and perhaps even one section of a detailed syllabus, so that there can be little doubt that the kind of approach to teaching we discussed in chapters 2 and 3 will create even greater demands for resources of all kinds, demands that no teacher can ignore or easily satisfy. New kinds of teaching demand new resources and the particular approaches that have been introduced in recent years demand both a greater quantity and a greater variety.

In order to obtain a clearer view of the kinds of resource that may be needed and a basis on which we can select among what is available, it may be helpful to begin by getting clear about the uses of resources and the purposes that they might help us to achieve. There would seem to be three main purposes that resources will be designed to serve. These three purposes we can look at separately but we must not lose sight of the fact that in practice they will be closely interrelated.

In the first place, resources have always been used by teachers as aids to motivation, as devices to stimulate the interest of the pupils. Few teachers can be unaware of the immediate transformation of the level of attention of any class, even in the most formal lesson, when an object is produced to illustrate a point that the teacher is making – a Roman nail found at Verulamium, a fossil, even a piece of coal or a lump of cheese. These aids are important in all lessons; they become vastly more important in a situation where we are trying to work from the interests of pupils. We have said elsewhere that the first task is to stimulate interest; this will be incredibly difficult to do successfully without a vast array of resources chosen for this purpose. Indeed, it was suggested earlier that one way of stimulating interest is to surround the pupils with resources of this kind and let them browse among them, explore them and find within them something that sparks them off. This would suggest that at this stage the resources may be more important than the teacher, whose first job is done when he has made a careful choice of resources and made them available to his pupils.

We must beware, of course, of overstimulating them so that they become merely excited and are not ready to settle down to the hard work that must follow. For once interest has been stimulated, as we have seen, the next task is to feed it and this is the second purpose of resources – to aid and promote learning once begun. Having gained some idea of the areas in which they want to work, pupils need to be able to start work as soon as possible. We suggested in chapter 2 that the teacher should have work-cards ready to enable them to get started without his personal help, so that he can devote his attention to those who for one reason or another are not ready to begin work on their own. He will also need suitable resource materials that they can start work on. Furthermore, having embarked on an enquiry, a project or a piece of work, pupils will need to be given access to sources of information that will enable them to work on it at an appropriate pace. We have already referred to the fact that interest will quickly be lost if it is not fed and in teaching through individual and group assignments it can only be fed by the provision of the right kinds of resource material. It is essential that this kind of material be available throughout the project so that the teacher does not need to cover the same ground several times with different groups and can save his time and energies for dealing with problems that must have his personal attention. It is important to remember too that material provided for pupils with this purpose in mind must also satisfy our first purpose, to maintain their interest and stimulate and give access to further interests. If a pupil has opened up a rich vein, we must provide him with the tools that will enable him to get all that is worth having from it and the incentive to keep working at it.

A third main purpose of resource material is to stimulate the imagination of pupils. In chapter 2 reference was made to the dangers of always seeing the individual assignment in terms of information gathering and of losing the opportunities that this kind of situation offers for engaging pupils in creative and imaginative activities. It would not be appropriate here to become involved in discussions of what we might mean by 'creative activities' or of the relative merits of this kind of activity and other elements of the curriculum,[1] but attention must be drawn to the concern that has been expressed in recent years about the over-emphasis in schools on fact-finding and fact-storing to the detriment of the development of creative abilities, and of the credit given to the convergent rather than the divergent thinker in the traditional structure of the education system. It has been felt not only that this results in an unbalanced education for some individuals, but also that it has serious implications for society which needs more creative people than the education system produces. The arguments here are strong. Clearly, for some teachers they will be of more direct and immediate relevance than for others, but few can ignore the demand that this places on them to be as aware of the development of the imagination of their pupils as of their intellect. Nor must we make the mistake of

1 For a critical discussion of this problem, see, for example, R. F. Dearden, *The Philosophy of Primary Education* (RKP, 1968), pp. 142 ff.

assuming that these two aspects of the development of pupils can be treated in isolation from each other. As we have just said, it is not possible in practice to distinguish the interrelated purposes of resource materials. We shall have cause to note again, when we come to look at the question of assessment in chapter 8, that there is an inevitable interrelationship between feeling and learning, between the affective and the cognitive, so that when we set out to stimulate the imagination of pupils and arouse their feelings we are at the same time promoting their learning; conversely, we cannot seek to promote intellectual learning without giving any thought to the emotional factors involved. To attend to this effectively, teachers must place a great deal of reliance on resource materials.

To help teachers with all aspects of their teaching there is nowadays a wealth of material available, some of it prepared directly for them by publishers and others, some of it available from the things we all come across in our everyday lives. Some of it is in straightforward graphic form – cuttings from newspapers, comics and colour supplements, posters and so on; some will be materials that can be looked at, handled and perhaps manipulated in various ways – rock samples, geometrical shapes and solids, models designed to demonstrate certain scientific principles; others again will be of a kind that will require special equipment for their use – audio- and video-tapes, films, film-strips and slides. Nor must we lose sight of the fact that places pupils might visit and people who might visit the school or be visited by groups of pupils can be important sources of learning. There is nothing that *prima facie* is not potentially a source of learning or an aid to teaching, so that teachers can become great collectors of junk. The profession has its Steptoes, as we all know, but some criteria of selection are needed if teachers are not to become buried under a mass of unused materials and certain conditions seem to follow from the basic purposes we have outlined.

A prime consideration is that the material offered to pupils should be the most interesting that is available. To some extent, decision on this is a matter for personal preference and judgement and, in any case, it will often be possible for children to select for themselves and teachers will have this very important feed-back to help them with their choices. One general principle, however, does seem important and can be offered as a broad guide to teachers choosing material. Preference should always be given to first-hand resources where they are available. A piece of bark will always be a better aid to learning than a picture of a piece of bark; a newspaper cutting on a particular topic will always be better than a statement about it prepared for use in the classroom; a visit from the local 'bobby' will always elicit more interest and learning than exhibiting his helmet, badges or truncheon. To say this is, of course, merely to draw attention to a general educational principle that applies in all teaching situations, but its importance in the selection of resource materials must not be forgotten.

A second vital point is that the resources we prepare for pupils should satisfy the educational criteria we discussed in the first chapters of this book. They should be related to the objectives of the project they are meant to serve; they are not to be seen merely as devices for keeping pupils busy, but as aids to the achievement of whatever objectives the teacher has or comes to have. They must ensure that the pupil is stretched; we have stressed the need to avoid undirected learning or a 'hobbies' approach and the resources we provide must make appropriate demands of each pupil. They should also be chosen with the development of understanding in mind; we have claimed that this, rather than the acquisition of knowledge, is the proper aim of education and the resources we choose should reflect this. Furthermore, if we believe that the road to education may be different for each individual pupil and that we should individualize our educational provision, they should reflect this too. Finally, we should not lose sight of the need to promote the kind of imaginative and creative work we have just been discussing.

A third important consideration is that resources to be used by the pupils themselves must be of a kind that they can use, for the most part, without help from the teacher. Obviously, this means first that they must be suited to the pupils' level of understanding in terms of the language in which they are expressed or the illustrations, diagrams and the like that they may contain. This in turn implies a great variety of materials and also a wide range of books, since not all pupils in a mixed-ability class will be able to profit from the same material. As we shall stress when we come to consider the slow learner and the non-reader in chapter 6, it means that it will be necessary to prepare our work-cards and many of our resources in a number of forms and at a number of different levels of complexity. This will be particularly important if it is our concern to take all pupils through the same syllabus. Non-readers, for example, or those whose skill in reading is very limited will need to have resources and 'work-cards' prepared for them in different media. Clearly, the audio-tape can have particular value here, but it may not be so easy for the pupil to use and this brings us to the second main consideration. Resources must be in such a form that they are readily accessible to the pupils. In many cases this may mean that they will have to be restricted to items that can be used directly without the aid of any special equipment, but teachers are increasingly coming to feel that since such equipment is now more readily available than it once was, its use should no longer be restricted to the teacher who can only use it in a mass showing to the whole class, but it should be made available for individual pupils or groups to use, as and when it seems appropriate for their work. The language laboratory is now an established part of the educational scene in many secondary schools. There is no evident reason why the advantages that language teachers have been able to gain from the use of new equipment by pupils should be denied to other teachers. A classroom devoted to individual or group learning can readily include areas for viewing video-tapes, film-strips, films or slides and for listening to audio-tapes, although in a team-teaching project it may be better to have each kind of machine in a different room. Furthermore pupils who are accustomed to operating television sets, radios and record-players in their homes and often tape-recorders, movie-cameras and projectors of various kinds too, can be trusted to operate similar machines in school – perhaps more than many teachers. It always comes as a surprise to see pupils handling such equipment at school, but it never strikes one as strange to see them with it in their own homes. Perhaps what is surprising is it's availability in school rather than its use by the pupils.

Some pupils, then, will know how to use equipment of this kind; the rest will need to be shown. This can be done quite easily by a teacher who knows his way around the basic educational hardware. This in turn highlights the fact that an introduction to the workings of educational technology is nowadays an essential part of any teacher's training. Whatever we feel about the desirability of allowing pupils to operate these machines themselves, there is no doubt that teachers must have this kind of expertise. It must also be stressed, however, that teachers need rather more than a course on how to work the machines; they also need a more extensive training in the uses and applications of educational technology and in the preparation of their own materials for use with the machines, since here again the first-hand item, prepared for a specific task, is infinitely preferable to the 'shop bought' model. Teachers trained in recent years should have been given this kind of training; older teachers will have had little preparation for work of this kind and their experiences of educational technology may have engendered in them a great suspicion of all such aids. They will need to be persuaded that there have been great advances in this field since the days when Olympic high-divers leapt gracefully feet-first from swimming bath to high-diving board and Mexican cowboys galloped at great speed rump-first across the pampas of South America to the accompaniment of a growling soundtrack which eventually brought everything to a complete standstill. The level of sophistication in educational technology is much higher now, as in fact many older teachers seem to have discovered, since there are indications of a greater use of educational technology by older teachers than by the younger ones.

In time, then, it must be hoped that the greater variety of resources now available to teachers can be made available also to pupils in this way. But it is also to be hoped that neither teachers nor pupils will be misled by the nature of these new developments into falling for gimmicks. The emphasis must remain on the educational aspects of educational technology and the technology must not be embraced for its own sake. Its advantages can only be evaluated in terms of its contribution to the advancement of the learning of the pupil and in relation to the contributions to be made by other kinds of resource. In particular, we must not forget the advantages of books, one of the oldest but still one of the most reliable and accessible of resources. In this connection it is interesting to note that where other resources have been made available to pupils an increased interest in books has seemed to result.

Whatever kinds of resource material the individual teacher favours and is able to use and make available to his pupils, there is no doubt that work with mixed-ability classes, and in particular work that is enquiry-based or interest-based, will make it essential that he amasses great quantities of material. A single project will require a great mass of material of all kinds; a team of teachers will collect even more. Much of this material will be of a kind that can be used over and over again with successive groups of pupils and, although it is obviously desirable that teachers should be continually adding new items and weeding out the outdated to ensure that it is always abreast of the times, it is clearly not good sense to start from scratch each time and develop entirely new resources for each project. Some method of storing material that has been collected is vital.

Most teachers will, of course, keep material that they feel has a value for the future in a cupboard and the whereabouts of each individual item in their heads, but in time one of two things will happen. Either they will go to the cupboard and fail to lay hands on the item they want, perhaps in a situation where a pupil or group of pupils is crying out for it, or they will one day open the cupboard door and be buried in a deluge of colour supplements, film-strips, slides, specimens, pictures of Hannibal crossing the Alps and other such bric-à-brac – an experience unpleasant to the teacher, although highly entertaining for the pupils if they happen to be around when it happens. It is at this point that the teacher realizes that he needs a resources bank or collection. For what converts a cupboard full of junk into a resources collection is the introduction of a system of indexing and storing which will ensure easy access to, and retrieval of, each individual resource item collected.

In the first instance, such a system need not be highly sophisticated.[2] The resources collection at my own college began with a few box files in a cupboard and a shoe box for the index cards.[3] It is enough to get hold of several boxes of a similar size, either purchased for the purpose or begged from a local grocer, so that items can be separated under broad headings. Some sort of simple card-index system will enable one to extend this and will help with the retrieval of items stored. A card for each item, on which is indicated first, the broad category it has been allocated to and, therefore, the box it is kept in and, secondly, a number to show its whereabouts in the box, is simple to prepare and, if kept in alphabetical order with other such cards, affords quick and ready access to any item. A further refinement of some value can be achieved by varying the colour of the index cards – for example, white for cuttings from newspapers and magazines, yellow for slides, pink for posters and charts and so on.

The introduction of a system such as this will bring immediate improvement and a feeling, for the most part justified, of being in control of things

2 For a more detailed discussion of the development of an indexing system through several levels of sophistication, see J. Hanson, *Ideas*, no. 19/20, 1971.

3 For an account of the development of the Goldsmiths' College Resources Collection, see J. Ellis, *Ideas*, no. 19/20, 1971.

again, but it does have serious limitations. Items will still be 'lost' or much time wasted in the retrieval process because of the difficulties of classification and the need for some form of cross-referencing. For example, a cutting from a colour supplement describing the plight of women and children in the Indo–Pakistan war might be classified under 'Women', 'Children', 'Family', 'Hunger', 'War', 'India' or 'Pakistan'. Whichever heading it is listed under, it will not be turned up by anyone looking for items on any of the other six topics, although it might be highly relevant to them. Furthermore, anyone looking for items concerned specifically with, say, 'Women in War', will waste time looking at a lot of items under both 'Women' and 'War' when in fact he is interested only in those that link both of these classifications together.

Some system of cross-referencing, therefore, becomes important at a very early stage in the development of a resources collection. One answer to this problem, and one favoured by many, is to keep several cards on each item and thus list it under all the appropriate headings, each card containing also an indication of the other headings under which the item is listed. A more sophisticated system is the optical-coincidence punch-card system. With this system a punch-card is prepared as an index card for each topic and item number 672, for example, which is our cutting about women and children in the Indo–Pakistan war, is recorded by a hole punched at square number 672 on all the relevant index cards – 'Women', 'Children', 'Family', 'Hunger', 'War', 'India' and 'Pakistan'. That 672 is an item relevant to the theme 'Women in War' or 'Women in War in India' will be quickly discovered when we take the index cards, 'Women' and 'War', and 'India' too if we wish, and place them on top of one another. The holes at number 672 will clearly coincide, indicating the relevance of this item, whereas items relevant to only one of these themes will not show up. Thus quick retrieval of only those items that are fully relevant to our particular purposes becomes possible. Equipment can be obtained for easy reading of these cards, but they can be read without elaborate equipment. Such a system is, of course, at a level of sophistication some way beyond the shoe box we started with. It is also seen by some to have drawbacks which outweigh its advantages. It is more complicated to run than the simple card-index system and it makes it very difficult to withdraw items from the collection when they become outdated, since although the holes in the punch-cards can be filled in or some other method of showing withdrawal used, this is not so easy as simply destroying the relevant card.

Whichever system is favoured, the crux of the problem is the categories that are used for classification. To a large extent, material should be classified under headings that are relevant to the courses or projects they will be required to serve. Since we are working from the assumption that the problem arises from the fact that masses of material have been collected already to deal with earlier projects, we can begin by saying that it should be classified under the headings under which it was first collected, since these clearly were the relevant points to the pupils then. A list of themes should be drawn up primarily on this basis, but such a list should always be open-ended so that other categories of classification can be added as and when they seem appropriate and necessary.

For a number of reasons, however, teachers would be well advised not to make such a system too idiosyncratic. So far, we have treated this problem as one that is of growing concern to the individual teacher facing up to the requirements of his mixed-ability class either within his own specialist subject or across a range of subjects he might be responsible for. As each teacher's collection of resources grows, however, it will prove uneconomical in every sense for every teacher to continue to develop his own collection and some kind of centralization will become essential. Furthermore, we have already seen how the new approaches to teaching that a mixed-ability form of organization makes necessary lead quickly to some form of team-teaching and this again makes it necessary to think of developing a joint resources centre which all members of the team can use. This kind of development must be borne in mind from the outset if a smooth transition is to be effected to a large and more central organization of resources, so that some generally agreed basis of classification is needed at the beginning.

Ultimately, such a resources centre must be closely linked with the school or college library and this development must also be kept in mind from the very beginning. Even in the early stages of a resources collection, there are enormous advantages in cataloguing not only items actually contained in the collection but also other relevant items to be found elsewhere. The inclusion of references to basic books in the school library is, therefore, a great asset. In this way, a link with the school library can and should be maintained throughout, so that there would seem to be certain advantages in adopting a system that is as compatible with the Dewey system of classification as is possible. This system of classification itself is not always the most helpful, since it was not designed for teaching purposes, and teachers must not allow themselves to be kept too strictly to it, but to keep as close to it as possible will help when the resources centre becomes a part of the school library.

When this happens, we will have progressed a long way from our shoe box and cupboard beginnings. For what we can now hope to have is a Resources Centre (note the transition to capital letters) in its own purpose-built accommodation. Such accommodation should include, in addition to storage space and places for looking at pictorial, written and other non-projected materials, booths for the viewing of projected materials of all kinds, slides, film-strips, films, records, audio- and video-tapes. It should also include facilities for making and reproducing items, since teachers need to be able to produce their own teaching and learning aids, or have them produced for them, and pupils need to be able to secure copies of items they may need in their work but of which the Centre may contain only reference copies – there is no point in loaning a precious copy of an article if this can be reprographed and the original retained in safe keeping.

Facilities for photocopying, typing, duplicating must be readily available, therefore, and there must also be provision for the recording of radio and television broadcasts and the preparation of other audio- and video-tapes, of films, slides, transparencies for use with the overhead projectors and any other aids to teaching and learning that teachers or pupils may need. Such provision may seem a long way off in most schools, but it is something to be worked for and a clear vision of what the future may bring will help to ensure that the early stages of the development of a resources collection are approached in a way that makes subsequent development along these lines as smooth as possible.

Most schools are still at an early stage in the development of their collections of resources, but since this is an area of growing need, many people have already moved into this field and offer ready-made collections or packs of resource materials on particular themes or areas of work. The Schools Council projects already referred to have seen the development of resources as an essential element in their work and have prepared resource packs for sale to schools.[4] Others too have been quick to see the need and to prepare collections of material for use by teachers in certain areas of work. Indeed, some publishers are seeing the need to divert some of their attention from the preparation of textbooks to the publication of packs of materials of this kind. All of these sources will provide the teacher with assistance in his basic task of feeding the educational appetite of his pupils and it must be stressed that for the most part such large-scale undertakings have the advantage of being based on wider research and experience than is possible for the individual teacher.

However, it must again be stressed that each school should develop its own individual collection suited to its own unique needs. What is generally available may be based on sound research and a resultant knowledge of general needs and may have much to offer the individual teacher, but the individual teacher has a knowledge of the individual pupils he is catering for as well as of his own teaching style and to rely entirely on material prepared for him by others is to lose the advantage that such personal knowledge affords. Furthermore, there are additional advantages to be gained from a situation in which the users of the collection are also contributors to it. For in addition to the fact that teacher-users can thus develop a highly personalized collection of material to assist their own teaching, there is no better guide to what is good resource material nor any better criterion of selection than the observation of what pupil-users do in fact use. Fundamentally, a resources collection should begin from the need to store what has been used by the pupils. There is nothing that is more 'first hand' than that and teachers should not lose sight of this fundamental point in their desire to provide more and more sophisticated material. Nor should

4 For each area of enquiry that material has been prepared for by the Humanities Curriculum Project packs containing twenty copies of each item for pupils, two teacher's sets, including handbooks, two copies of an introductory booklet on the Project and one set of tapes are available from Heinemann Educational Books Ltd.

pupils always be 'spoon fed'. There is much to be learnt by being required to do one's own research in the full sense of the word, to find one's own source material instead of merely using other people's, and there is no greater assurance of the value of one's work than to see material one has obtained entering the resources collection for future generations to use.

There can also be profit in encouraging pupils to assist with the actual classification and indexing of materials. It is always a temptation, of course, to take advantage of the cheap labour pupils can provide, but it is possible to justify employing them in this way on educational grounds. In a College of Education this work should certainly be done by students, since this is another skill they should learn in their preparation for teaching, but this is not the only advantage. The problems of collecting, sorting and classifying can be seen to have a certain educational value in themselves, since a good deal of careful and analytical thinking must go into them. To paraphrase Rousseau, 'While he thinks himself a librarian, he is becoming a philosopher.'

The provision of resources for learning, then, is another major task for the teacher of a mixed-ability class and perhaps more complex when considered in detail than it appears to be on a first and rather superficial view. The important thing is to be clear about the general principles upon which one's own collection will be based and on the techniques that should be used to ensure that no opportunities for future development on whatever scale are lost. If the individual teacher is clear about these, then he can develop a system that can be adapted to any level of sophistication of materials, equipment or indexing and which will help him with the task of providing the right kind of education for each of his pupils.

Chapter 6

Slow Learners and Non-readers

There is little doubt that the aspect of mixed-ability teaching that worries teachers most is the presence in mixed-ability classes of slow learners and non-readers for whom appropriate provision needs to be made. Indeed, many teachers have based their arguments for streaming on the need to group such pupils separately in order to make it easier to provide for them[1] and many have come to feel that this is an area of specialism that should be left to those specially equipped to deal with it. However, it is apparent that to separate such pupils from their fellows is to exacerbate rather than to alleviate their difficulties and those of their teachers and it is for this reason as much as any that the mixed-ability form of organization is being introduced. We must carefully consider therefore, how the teacher can best take advantage of the opportunities it offers him in this sphere. The mixed-ability class gives the teacher the chance to let all pupils work at the pace most suited to them and at the level most suited to them, so that exceptionally gifted pupils, who can be equally a source of problems to the teacher – not least those problems that arise when he is trying to educate pupils who may be brighter than himself – can be catered for within it perhaps more adequately than they can be catered for in a streamed class. The slow learner does, however, provide problems in the mixed-ability situation. He will probably lack the confidence and some of the very basic skills that might be felt essential to individual or group assignment work at secondary level, he may well have acquired, by the time he reaches the secondary school, certain emotional and social problems which the teacher will need to attend to and he may, as a result of persistent failure, if he has been made to feel conscious of it, have become a problem pupil, providing the teacher with problems of behaviour and control. Such a pupil can be troublesome even in his first year at a secondary school and, unless a change is made in the nature and quality of his educational experience, he will, as any teacher knows, give particular trouble in the last year of his schooling. While it is also true that the gifted pupil can be difficult if bored, to a large extent he can be dealt with by overcoming his boredom; it is the slow learners that the teacher needs most help with in the mixed-ability class.

Some general points need to be made about slow learners[2] before we can begin to consider how we might cater for them in a mixed-ability class. To begin with, it is important to be clear about the extent of the problem. It is difficult to be precise about this, not least because of the problems that surround the establishment of adequate criteria of measurement in such a

1 See, for example, B. Jackson, *Streaming: an Education System in Miniature* (RKP, 1964), p. 32.
2 For a full discussion of the education of slow-learning pupils see A. E Tansley and R. Gulliford, *The Education of Slow Learning Children* (RKP, 1960).

problematic area. There is general agreement, however, that whatever criteria one employs, about 10 per cent of pupils will be found to be significantly backward in the basic skills of language and number.[3] Furthermore, although the figure will vary from school to school and from neighbourhood to neighbourhood, there can be few non-selective secondary schools which do not contain a significant number of non-readers. The problem, then, is widespread and is one that every teacher of a mixed-ability class will experience.

The most important point to be kept in mind when looking at this problem is the changes that have occurred in recent years in the view taken by psychologists of the nature of intelligence. The old concept of intelligence as a fixed and unchangeable level of general ability with which the individual is born and which is determined therefore, entirely by nature has given way to the view that, although nature may place certain end limits on its potential development, nevertheless intelligence can be developed by education, that childhood experiences can promote or retard its development and that nurture is at least as important here as nature. This is what Sir Edward Boyle had in mind when, as Minister of Education, he prefaced the Newsom Report[4] with the now famous dictum that 'all children should have an equal opportunity of acquiring intelligence'. This is one of the basic reasons for the change to mixed-ability classes. It is felt wrong to label children at an early age, to 'discover their IQ' and offer them an education appropriate to it, since there is evidence to suggest that nothing determines a child's IQ so effectively as the teacher's own view of what it is and the expectations that result from the teacher's view of it.[5] This is the 'self-fulfilling prophecy' to which we have already referred. If we only demand a 'C' stream level of work from pupils, this is all we will get and we will not then be giving them the opportunity to 'acquire intelligence'. If intelligence can be developed, there is scope for the teacher.

There is similar encouragement for the teacher in the views of those psychologists such as Piaget and Bruner who have for the most part abandoned this rather passive view of intelligence and have concerned themselves with a study of intellectual development,[6] since this has led to a view of education as being concerned to accelerate intellectual growth rather than to purvey information and has taken it as a basic assumption that intellectual development can be promoted by the right kind of educational provision. Again there is scope for the teacher. The mixed-ability class is one way of helping him to use this scope.

Another reason why streaming has come to be regarded as an inefficient method of grouping pupils is that it assumes that it is possible to generalize about slow learning and thus it inhibits the making of more subtle distinc-

---

3 See DES pamphlet no. 46, *Slow Learners at School* (HMSO, 1964), p. 18.
4 *Half Our Future* (HMSO, 1963).
5 See D. A. Pidgeon, *Expectation and Pupil Performance* (NFER, 1970).
6 For a full discussion of this and related points, see D. Elkind, *Children and Adolescents* (OUP, 1970), chapter 8.

tions between different types of learning difficulty. A child may be a slow learner in only one or two areas, but, if placed in the 'C' stream, he is offered a 'C' stream diet in all areas and is thus undernourished in most. A distinction needs to be made between the kind of slow learning that is the result of what appears to be a limited intellectual potential and that which results from a failure to make effective use of an ability that seems to be present. In other words, one must be aware of the different types of provision needed for those pupils who are 'dull' and reveal a limited ability or potential in all areas and for those who are 'retarded', who seem to be underachieving or underfunctioning in particular areas, when their work in those areas is compared with what is known of their general potential. The latter require help that can be truly described as 'remedial', since a particular and, one hopes, temporary deficiency is to be made good and the provision of such help can be seen to be possibly a short-term measure to which they may respond quite quickly. The former need to be viewed in a long-term way, since the problem here is not to put right some temporary deficiency, but to provide them with a complete education, whose objectives are the same as for all pupils, but which must be developed in a way that makes best use of their strengths and must be designed to make the most of their limited potential. However, although each of these groups needs a different kind of provision, we should never be in too much of a hurry to place individuals in one group or the other, since once we have classified a particular pupil as 'dull', we will be inclined to restrict the demands we make of him and we should always be reluctant to do this, since, as we have seen, teacher expectancy is a key factor in the achievement of all pupils. We need to look carefully into each case to discover the reasons for particular instances of slow learning and we need, therefore, to have some idea of the kinds of factor that seem to cause slow learning.

Clearly, limitation of intellectual potential is one major cause of slow learning, but there are other reasons which are often more crucial. We have already referred in discussing the grouping of pupils to the importance of the emotional and social environment in which pupils learn for their intellectual progress. There is clear evidence[7] that slow learning is often due to emotional and social deprivation. The absence of a mother's love in the early years of life may be as serious a disadvantage to the individual's subsequent intellectual development as we know it is for his emotional development and the continued absence of a secure and stable background in the home will reinforce this initial disadvantage. The educational level of the home too will affect a child's rate of progress at school. The education of the parents themselves and their attitudes to education, the kind of language used in the home, the presence or absence of books, papers, records and so on will have serious implications for the child's 'readiness' for education and his ability to profit from what the school offers him, since factors of this kind will govern his level of motivation and the skills and attitudes he brings to school with him. The pupil's physical capacities

7 See for example A. E. Tansley and R. Gulliford, op. cit., *passim.*

must also be taken into account, since they too have a direct bearing on his educational progress. At one level we must be on the look-out for physical disabilities such as partial deafness or sight difficulties that can be root causes of slow learning if not detected in time, but at another level, we should also be aware of the implications of physical maturity for the intellectual development of all pupils. A certain neurological maturation must take place before the individual can learn certain things and there is a clear link between the kind of intellectual development analysed by Piaget and others and the physical development of the individual. This seems to be particularly significant at the adolescent stage where the pupil who is late to reach puberty is also likely to be a late developer intellectually. Finally, we must not forget the ways in which the school itself can, and often does, promote slow learning. The school can create emotional barriers to learning as readily as the home can; it can destroy the individual's motivation to learning and the confidence with which he approaches it; it can offer a social environment that militates against effective learning at the academic level as well as the social.

One of the more obvious ways in which the school can do this disservice to those of its pupils who have learning difficulties would seem to be by segregating them from their fellows in a permanent way which labels them as different, inferior, difficult, ineducable, non-examinable or whatever. Nothing can do their social and emotional development more harm and nothing can do their intellectual development less good. It has often been said that if nothing succeeds like success, then conversely nothing fails like failure. It is often the practice, based on the very best of intentions, to put such pupils into separate classes, to provide them often with highly skilled and sympathetic teachers and even to give them a greater share of the school's financial resources. While such a practice is obviously motivated by a desire to do what is best for such pupils, it is misguided and it is for this reason more than any other that schools are moving towards a mixed-ability form of organization. There are very good psychological and social reasons for not segregating such pupils in this way and for allowing them to work with others on as many common activities as possible. The dividing line between the provision of special treatment and the establishment of a ghetto is very narrow. Slow learners should not be singled out, their difficulties should not be highlighted and they should not be made to feel that they have no valuable and valued contribution to make to the life and work of the school.

If this is the thinking behind the move towards a mixed-ability form of organization, it would seem a contradiction of that thinking to use the individual assignment approach as a device for singling out the less able for remedial treatment at a time when the others are pursuing their own individual or group assignments. One of the strongest arguments for this method, as we have seen, is that it allows every pupil to work at his own pace and at his own level, and since, as we have also seen, learning difficulties cannot be generalized and each case of slow learning is unique, the individual assignment approach would seem to be most appropriate as a means of diagnosing and dealing with each individual's personal educational problems without viewing him as a member of a special group requiring special 'compensatory' or 'remedial' treatment.

Clearly, such pupils will need remedial help in some areas, perhaps especially in basic reading skills and we must not ignore the development of these important basic skills. All pupils, however, will need some remedial help. Some bright pupils will need remedial help even with their reading. Few of us are not slow learners at something and slow learning must be seen in relation to specific areas of work and skills, not as a general disability. Viewed like this, remedial work can be seen to be required by all pupils and a programme must be devised for the mixed-ability class that will enable all pupils to obtain this kind of remedial help. The timetable, therefore, must include remedial periods as well as blocks of time for work on individual and group assignments. This will, however, be provision for all to make good their deficiencies, the pupil who is having trouble with quadratic equations no less than the one who cannot cope with the four rules of arithmetic, and it will happen for all at set times in the week. It may well be that the problem of the non-reader is more intractable than this and that a more intensive programme is needed, perhaps a crash course at a Reading Centre outside the school, to get to grips effectively with this difficulty. If this is so, then the appropriate provision should be made and a suitable amount of time allocated for this purpose. Time allocated for individual and group assignment work, however, should not be seen by the teacher as an opportunity to mount an intensive remedial campaign on his slow learners or non-readers, except in so far as it gives scope for encouragement and enhanced motivation or provides cues for the teaching of basic skills. To do this is to deprive the other pupils of their share of his attention, to make the slow learners unduly conscious of their difficulties and to deprive them of the opportunities and advantages that individual and group assignments offer to all pupils and to them in particular. For the advantages that have been claimed elsewhere in this book for such work are particularly important in the education of slow learners.

In the first place, it has been argued that when pupils are allowed to work at their own pace and level, and perhaps also in pursuit of their own interests, there are great gains in motivation and incentive to work and to learn. This is precisely the kind of gain we are looking for in the education of the slow learner. If he can be allowed to do what interests him, if he can be encouraged to take on what he can cope with, if we play to his strengths rather than his weaknesses, then we can reasonably hope to achieve a level of motivation that may give us rather more chance of doing something for such a pupil than we have often had in the past. If his attitude towards school and teachers improves as a result of this so that he ceases to offer behavioural difficulties, something of value will have been gained; but we can hope to gain even more if we succeed in building up his confidence in this way. We mentioned in chapter 2 the stress placed by psychologists such as Piaget on the part played by intrinsic motivation in intellectual development. Allowing the slow learner to work from his own interests is one way in which we may hope to develop intrinsic motivation and thus assist his intellectual development.

A second advantage that has been claimed for individual and group assignment work, especially when it is also interest- and enquiry-based, is the opportunities it offers for the promotion of creative work of all kinds. Again, such work offers special advantages to the slow learner. It is often claimed that such pupils learn primarily by doing. This is probably true of most pupils but is perhaps particularly important to those with learning difficulties. Drama, movement, art and handwork of all kinds are important to all pupils but their importance to the slow learner is vital. Such pupils are probably experiencing the greatest difficulty in expressing themselves through the written word and perhaps the spoken word too; reading and writing difficulties will present them with real problems of communication. Other media can offer them a means of expression denied them through language. I have myself seen groups of fifteen-year-old girls, who were about to leave school with little to show for their ten-year sojourn there, expressing through dance ideas of a complexity that would have been impossible for them to express through words. Opportunities for self-expression of this kind will contribute also to their emotional development since their feelings need not remain bottled up inside or manifest themselves in bad behaviour but can be channelled into socially acceptable modes of expression through such art forms. Work of this kind will also promote learning in other fields, since, if satisfaction is achieved, they will want to talk about what they have done and might even be persuaded to write about it; they might also be led by a skilled teacher from such activities into others that arise naturally from them.

Furthermore, these are areas in which the confidence of such pupils can be developed because they can perhaps achieve something worthwhile here. There are those who, although experiencing difficulty with reading and writing, reveal real talent for painting, modelling, dancing or acting. If they have such strengths, the teacher should take advantage of them. Even those who do not possess talent in these directions, however, can be helped by an imaginative teacher to achieve real success in these areas. Art does not have to be conceived as painting or sculpting; it can be seen as the creation of a 'montage' out of a variety of materials. Dance does not have to be interpreted in a strict balletic form; it can be viewed as free expressive movement. Drama need not be restricted to the acting of plays written by others; it can be the expression of one's own feelings through mime or improvised dialogue. In short, although all of these areas can provide opportunities for some pupils to reveal and develop great skills and although it should be the teacher's aim to enable pupils to develop these skills to the highest level in order to achieve the greatest scope for self-expression and satisfaction, skilled performance is not always an essential and all pupils can achieve some satisfaction in them.

A third main area in which it has been argued that individual and group assignment work offers advantages to pupils is that of social learning, which, as we have seen, also has its effects on academic learning. Again, this is the kind of advantage that the slow learner most has need of, since, as we have also seen, if his slow learning is not the result of the social climate of his home or the school itself, it will certainly be a potential cause of the development of certain social or anti-social attitudes. His social education must, therefore, be handled very carefully. We have stressed that the move to mixed-ability groups implies a move away from competition towards cooperation as a prime educational principle. The slow learner needs a cooperative rather than a competitive atmosphere in which to work if anyone does. Competition can only draw attention to his deficiencies and too much of that will cause him to become disheartened. A cooperative atmosphere, on the other hand, can do much to build his confidence by showing him that his work is worthwhile, that it is valued by others as adding something of value to a joint undertaking and is thus as worthy of respect as the work of the more gifted pupils. Only in this way can we hope to promote his social learning and avoid the development of emotional difficulties. The emotional development of all pupils requires the teacher's careful attention but that of slow learners requires particular attention since, as a general rule, their emotional development is most at risk. To have a mental age of twelve at a chronological age of sixteen is not to have an emotional age of twelve. It is, however, to be in danger of developing serious emotional problems. These problems of social and emotional development may be especially important in the final year at school, since it is at this age that the adolescent tends to be at his most 'emotional' and at this time that he is becoming socially aware and needs to be enabled and encouraged to make contributions at a number of levels that can be seen to be socially valuable. It is for this reason that many schools have found it helpful to engage pupils in their final year in various kinds of community service. Such activities are to the advantage of the community but the one who really profits from them is the pupil. They are advantageous to all pupils but particularly so to the slow learner. If teachers are not aware of these needs and do not cater for them, they can expect the slow learner, especially in his last year of school, to give them hell, as so many of them do.

In general, what is being asserted here is that remedial education, or whatever we wish to call the education of slow learners, is not to be seen simply as a matter of providing additional instruction. Rather, it is a matter of approaching their total education in a different frame of mind, of seeing the need to create the right social and emotional climate for them to work in and of building up their confidence in themselves by playing to their strengths, encouraging them to do the things they can and ensuring that their achievements in these fields are valued by us and by their fellows. Clearly, this requires the mixed-ability class, and within the mixed-ability class it can best be achieved not by singling them out for special provision but by providing for them along with the rest in a situation where each pupil is working as part of a group or sub-group on an assignment suited to his abilities.

However, a weather eye does need to be kept on them. It was suggested when we discussed the grouping of pupils that particular attention would need to be given to the slow learners in this process to ensure that they would be accepted by the groups they joined and would have a genuine contribution to make to them. There are two aspects of this. In the first place, it has been stressed that the social development of these pupils may be particularly troublesome and teachers must keep their fingers on that pulse. Secondly, a careful watch must be kept on the nature of the contributions they are making to the work of a group to ensure that these contributions really are worthwhile and likely to help towards an improvement in their own learning. Teachers must also remember that the slow learner will have more trouble than most in adjusting to the bustling atmosphere of the classroom in which pupils are working on their own assignments. He will have less confidence than most to strike out on his own in this way and will need more support than most in doing so. As we saw in chapter 4, he will also need more help than most in making the social relationships necessary for working in this way. For all of these reasons the teacher must be particularly conscious of his slow learners and of how they are fitting into the pattern of work and of social relationships within his class.

So far it has been argued that the individual approach to education that seems to be implied by the move towards a mixed-ability form of organization can cater for the slow learner as well as any other pupil and that, far from depriving him of the advantages of working in this way, we must see these advantages as having a particular application to his learning difficulties. We must now look at the position of the non-reader, who would seem to present a teacher with particular problems since he lacks the basic skill to handle work-cards and most resources and it might be asked how he can be expected to take on his own individual assignment.

It would seem, in the first place, that if our case for the advantages of this approach is a valid one, we should be as reluctant to deprive the non-reader of these advantages as we are to deprive the slow learner of them. In fact, much the same reasoning would seem to apply here as we saw applied in the case of pupils with more general learning difficulties. We must remember that difficulties with reading, like all learning difficulties, can be the result of organic factors, of physical or neurological disabilities, but they are at least as likely to be due to environmental and emotional factors, elements in the pupil's experience at home or at school which have created blocks to his learning, so that even pupils of above average ability can be seen experiencing difficulties in learning basic skills such as reading. We saw, when considering slow-learning pupils in general, that the solution to difficulties that arise from factors of this kind is not only to make provision for additional instruction, since that, although important, is to attempt to deal only with the symptoms; it is rather to try also to get at the causes of the disability by creating a secure and stable environment in the school and in the classroom in which the pupil can work and through which his confidence can be built up and by keeping a particularly close watch on his social and emotional development, doing all that we can to make it as smooth as possible.

If this is a correct view of the problem and if we are right in claiming the social and emotional advantages for individual and group assignment work we have described, then it would seem unwise and undesirable to exclude non-readers from such work. For they, perhaps more than any other pupils, need the advantages that such an approach can bring. Obviously, as we have already suggested, they will need to be given intensive remedial help with their reading problems, but this should not be done at the expense of the opportunities that can be offered them for working on what they can do and possibly can do well, since to do this might well have the opposite effect to the one intended – it might merely aggravate the social and emotional factors that may lie behind the reading difficulties. If nothing else, these pupils can be given, via an individual assignment suited to their abilities, a rest from the hounding they sometimes get as non-readers from Monday morning to Friday afternoon in a traditional curriculum. For inability to read and write is a disadvantage that is highlighted in almost every curriculum subject. Individual assignment work should be seen as a chance to give them a break from this, to play to what strengths they have, as we have already said, and to try in this way to attend to their social and emotional development, which is both important in itself and can have the added advantage of making the way easier for their subsequent intellectual development. They also need the advantages that can come from the social relationships that develop through working with others on group projects. The practice of attaching non-readers to other groups to work in this way is well established in many junior schools and it is obviously a practice that teachers at secondary level would do well to emulate, not least in the final year where emotional difficulties are likely to erupt in serious behavioural problems.

Working in this way should also lead to gains in incentive and motivation, as we have suggested before, and since inability to read may stem from the absence of any incentive towards acquiring this skill, there is some hope that in certain cases the development of interests through individual assignments may lead to an increased level of motivation towards learning to read. It must be remembered that it is not only books that offer opportunities for reading or require this skill to be understood. Non-readers can be led into acquiring this skill by way of newspapers and magazines and also by way of time-tables, road signs, labels on foodstuffs and other household commodities, recipes in cookery books and many other such sources. There is scope for developing an interest in reading by this kind of route in individual and group assignment work. However, these pupils are non-readers and, although we may hope to build up their confidence and interest in this way, we must consider how they can be catered for by individual and group assignments.

In the first place, we will need to be particularly careful to develop resource material that they can use. It is obviously vital, therefore, that we think of resources in terms other than those of books, pamphlets and other written materials. It is for the non-reader in particular that we need to develop other kinds of resource. We suggested, when we were discussing in chapter 5 the provision of resources, that we should prepare tapes for non-readers instead of work-cards and that we should have ready as many resources that can be used without reading skills as we can obtain or make. The aim of individual and group assignment work is to make the pupil independent of the teacher and, if the teacher is not to spend an unfair proportion of his time with the non-readers and thus neglect those pupils who can read, he must be prepared to help the non-readers to become independent by taping material himself and making other provision of such resource material as they can use. Furthermore, this can help in the development of their reading skills too, since they can be given a written version of all or some of what is on the tape and can follow it as the tape is played.

Nor should we assume that printed matter cannot be used by non-readers. Although we are speaking of these pupils as non-readers, they will in fact be backward readers at various stages in the development of their reading skills. What is needed, therefore, as suggested in chapter 5, is the provision of the same resource material at several different levels of complexity to cater for the different levels of reading skill that we will find in any mixed-ability class. If we do this successfully, only the complete non-reader will be unable to cope with the written material we have and he can be catered for by the provision of tapes and other kinds of resource as we have just suggested.

Furthermore, it has already been suggested that such pupils can be employed as illustrators in a group project or contributing in some other way that does not entail reading or writing. They can also perform a very useful function, valued by their colleagues and giving them a sense of having something important to contribute, if they are encouraged to take responsibility for the use of some of the hardware the group may need. To operate a film-strip or slide projector, a tape-recorder or a camera requires skill of a different kind and this is the kind of contribution such children can initially be encouraged to make. I have myself seen pupils' attitudes to school and to teachers transformed by being given this kind of responsibility. One pupil in particular, I remember, a fifteen-year-old in his last year at school, who was a serious threat to the safety of teacher and pupils alike, until the tape-recorder was put into his care and he was given responsibility for all recording. Such pupils need to feel valued, as we all do.

We must beware, however, of appearing to suggest that such pupils should be used in group projects as handmaidens or attendants, assisting in the development of the ideas and the work of other, brighter pupils. As we stressed earlier in this chapter, educational objectives should be the same for all pupils and we must not willingly accept different objectives for our teaching of slow learners or non-readers. This is one reason why it is necessary to prepare similar resources at different levels of complexity, to ensure that they can be given similar work to do. It may be expedient in many cases to devise useful jobs for them of the kind we have just discussed, in order to secure their acceptance by a group, to build their confidence or even to keep them busy and ensure their good behaviour, but we must never let this cause us to lose sight of the fact that in the end our real concern should be with their education and whatever devices we employ they should always be seen as subservient to this end which is common to all pupils.

A third major consideration for the teacher, which again applies to all pupils but perhaps particularly to non-readers, is the importance of providing opportunities for the development of spoken language. As the Newsom Report[8] told us, 'Inability to speak fluently is a worse handicap than inability to read or write. . . . Personal and social adequacy depend on being articulate.' We might go further and claim that the development of the pupil's skill with spoken language will also lead to an improvement in his control over the written word. Children's language skills do not improve merely by the performance of written exercises. They improve as much, and in the early stages of language development considerably more, through opportunities to talk to others about what they have done and about what they are planning to do and how they intend to set about it. Language will develop by its use in expressing ideas that are important to the learner and will develop, therefore, by being used to describe activities and interests the pupil is engaged on. It can, therefore, be promoted by the kinds of activity associated with individual and group assignments, if teachers are conscious of its importance and prepared to provide opportunities for it. Formal reporting back to the class of progress made and of future plans has its place here and one should not discourage the non-reader from acting as spokesman for a group if he wishes to, but opportunities for informal discussion are probably of more value to all pupils and especially to those with reading problems. It is in this kind of area that the mixed-ability class and the mixed-ability group within the class offers particular advantages, for there can be little possibility for development of language skills if all members of the group are at roughly the same level of linguistic competence and proficiency. It is in a mixed-ability group, where the pupil who can express himself more easily must work to communicate with his less fluent fellows and they in turn can develop by their contact with those more fluent than themselves, that improvement can be hoped for in every pupil's linguistic ability.

A further way in which an incentive towards learning to read might be

8 *Half Our Future* (HMSO, 1963), para. 467.

created and a basis provided for some written and oral work is through the creative activities discussed elsewhere and the kind of community service work recommended earlier as suitable for slow learners in general, particularly in their last years at school. Both of these things, however, have an equal value for all pupils and, although their value as starting-points for reading and other learning may be greater for slow learners and non-readers, we must again be wary of appearing to suggest that these opportunities should be provided only for such pupils. We will need to discuss these points more fully when we come to consider the final years of schooling in chapter 8.

A final word must be said about the correction of such written work as the non-reader may be encouraged to produce by the teacher's efforts in the individual and group assignment situation. He must not be disheartened and discouraged by having every error indicated. After all, we will have had to work hard to build up his confidence and interest to the point where he has produced this work; we do not want to destroy the fruits of that by a too liberal use of a red pencil. Such work must be seen as a growth point, as an opportunity to lead the pupil on further, and we should, therefore, only draw his attention to errors we feel can now be corrected as the next stage of that growth. We should mark to encourage not to discourage and should bear in mind the development of the individual's ability to communicate rather than to spell or punctuate.

The slow learner and the non-reader must, then, be seen as an integral part of a mixed-ability class and not as a special case requiring separate treatment. If this is so, all teachers need to be prepared both to understand and to cater for slow learning and non-reading. All need the understanding necessary to be able to teach reading as a basic skill. It is a mistake to assume that this can be left to the infant or even to the junior teacher. There are enough non-readers in secondary schools to make this a serious problem for every teacher there. Furthermore, all will need an understanding of the nature of reading and the nature of the reading difficulties children suffer from. Even the subject specialist needs this kind of understanding if he is to provide his pupils with the kind of reading material they can profit from. This will be especially important in his teaching of mixed-ability classes since he must be able to choose a variety of reading materials suited to the needs of different individuals or groups across the whole range of ability. It is apparent that some pupils experience reading difficulties in certain subjects only and this puts an onus on the teacher of a subject to acquire this kind of understanding of the nature of reading in order to be able to discover why this should be so with certain of his own pupils in his own subject area.

Finally, few teachers would deny that most of the difficulties they have with control of their classes and the behaviour of certain pupils stems from the slow learners and non-readers. In a streamed school the 'C' stream has always been more difficult to handle than the 'A' stream and '4C' has been the death of many a teacher. The move to mixed-ability classes can be seen in terms of a philosophy of 'divide and rule'; it should be seen as an attempt to get to the roots of this difficulty and cure it by providing these slow learners with opportunities to do something valuable and constructive alongside the other children. If teachers do not succeed in helping them to take advantage of these opportunities, the behavioural problems will continue and the change will have been largely wasted.

Chapter 7

Teacher–Pupil Relationships

'When those you rule are unruly, look to your rule.' This, if not one of the more amusing, is certainly among the more significant of the sayings attributed to Confucius. Although there are pupils whom Confucius himself would find it difficult to handle, most problems of control in schools arise from the teacher–pupil relationships that the school and its individual teachers generate and these in turn depend to a considerable extent on the methods of control and the patterns of organization adopted. It would seem reasonable to assume, then, that a change in the organization of the school such as the introduction of mixed-ability classes will have major implications for the discipline within the school, and that if a mixed-ability form of organization is an improvement, it will lead to a corresponding improvement in the disciplinary situation and an alleviation of problems of control.

It would be a mistake, of course, to assume that all the school's and the teacher's problems are solved as soon as streaming is abandoned and mixed-ability classes are established. In the earlier chapters of this book it has been the aim to make it clear to teachers that they must work harder than ever to make this change work as well as to suggest some of the ways in which they may set about this task. Mixed-ability classes provide teachers with greater scope and with improved opportunities but the onus is on the teacher to take advantage of the opportunities offered. Similarly, it would be a mistake to assume that with the introduction of mixed-ability classes all problems of discipline and control disappear as if by magic. Indeed one can see that in one sense this kind of change creates more scope for misbehaviour and makes the teacher's task of controlling his class more difficult, since if pupils are to spend a lot of time working independently, they will need to talk and to move about the classroom and perhaps even the school building with some freedom and will of necessity be left much more to themselves, to work or not to work, than in a traditional class teaching situation. Potentially, then, there would seem to be dangers here that the teacher should be aware of.

On the other hand, there is some evidence to suggest[1] that a move to a mixed-ability form of organization is more usually accompanied by noticeable improvements in behaviour and a reduction in the problems of discipline and control. It has been noted that pupils' attitudes to school become more positive, that many of them cease to be difficult and that this improvement permeates all aspects of their work. In schools where they have been given a limited opportunity to work in mixed-ability situations, pursuing their own interests and investigations for only a part

1 See, for example, B. Kaye and R. Rogers, *Group Work in Secondary Schools* (OUP, 1968), pp. 68–9.

of the working week, improvements have been detected in their attitudes to work not only in that situation but also in the more conventional lessons they continued to have at other times. I have myself heard comments to this effect from teachers who were basically opposed to the 'nonsense' of interest and enquiry methods and reluctant to find any good in them. Again we must stress, however, that this is not an inevitable concomitant of the change; it is the result of the way in which teachers use the advantages the change gives them to develop more productive relationships with their pupils. That there are such advantages there is no doubt and to use them it is necessary to understand the form they take.

We must first of all take note of the fact that the move to a mixed-ability form of organization removes certain factors that seem to be productive of behavioural problems. It was said in chapter 6 that slow learners, when grouped together in a 'C' stream or a remedial class, can present the teacher with more discipline problems than most classes. Few teachers can fail to be aware of this and all will know only too well of the difficulties such classes can create in their final year of schooling. Nor should any teacher be surprised that pupils who have always experienced failure at school should want to fight the system and their teachers as representatives of it. There is after all no reason why we should expect such pupils to behave any differently from, for example, supporters or even directors of football teams which are unsuccessful. As we said before, nothing fails like failure. Like horses presented to fences too big for them to jump, slow-learning pupils, if not properly handled, will take any action necessary to avoid the disaster they know will follow if they do try to face up to the impossible demands being made of them. Unstreaming will ensure that such pupils are not gathered in what have been called 'sink' classes and will thus avoid a clear labelling of them as failures. It can also ensure that they are enabled to undertake valuable work at their own level. In this way it will remove one of the prime sources of behavioural problems and provide the teacher with a situation in which his attempts to establish good relationships with his pupils are not doomed to failure from the outset.

A second source of behavioural problems which is removed by the introduction of unstreaming, or at least by the individualized learning with which we have argued it should be associated, is the alienation of many pupils from the content of their learning. The concept of alienation has a long and complex history spanning the last two centuries, but basically it is a term whose use implies that a man-made creation achieves a pseudo-life of its own and begins to control man who created it. Thus Feuerbach, Marx and others have described man as alienated in relation to religion, government, work and so on and have seen this as an unhappy and 'unnatural' condition, productive of friction and in some cases ultimately of revolution. It is not uncommon for pupils to experience the same kind of alienation in relation to the traditional school curriculum or any curriculum that is totally teacher-directed. For a gap is created between their out-of-school interests and what they are required to involve themselves in inside the school, between the values exemplified in their own interests and those of their family and friends and the values implicit in the curriculum devised by the school. We might express this differently by using the terminology of A. N. Whitehead[2] and speaking of the knowledge they are being required to assimilate as a body of 'inert ideas' which in no way become a part of them but remain for ever separate, acquired, inactive and without real meaning for them. Again, this will be more commonly the experience of the slow learner; it will also be the experience of the pupil who comes from the kind of home in which the cultural background is very different from that implicit in the school curriculum; but to a greater or less degree it will be the experience of all pupils presented with a curriculum that comes entirely from outside them. It is also a phenomenon that is easily recognizable as a source of behavioural problems. As such, it is largely removed by the introduction of individual and group assignment methods, since even where these are mainly teacher-directed there is some element of pupil choice in them, a greater sense of pupil involvement and a higher level of motivation.

A further advantage of pupil-choice in relation to discipline and control is that it removes some of the need for compulsion that is so often a source of difficulty in dealing with children, and particularly with adolescents. Nobody likes to be forced to do anything: to be forced is to be deprived of the freedom we all value and, while one would not want to claim that compulsion is never necessary, it is to be avoided whenever possible in the interests of harmonious relationships. Compulsion is also at variance with the individual approach we have argued is essential in the teaching of mixed-ability classes and for this reason too is unlikely to lead to the successful handling of such groups of pupils. It is perhaps particularly to be deplored when applied to aspects of the pupil's life that have little or no relevance to his education. A case may be made on educational grounds for the claim that all pupils should be compelled to study mathematics; it may even be possible to produce the same kind of case for compulsory games, although one would want to look very carefully at its arguments, its presuppositions and especially the programme it was being produced to support; it is difficult to envisage, however, the kind of educational argument that could be adduced to justify an insistence on particular forms of dress or appearance or compulsory conformity to any norms in the notoriously fickle and changeable realm of fashion. If we really believe in individuality, in autonomy and personal freedom, in fact in education as a process that can be distinguished from indoctrination, conditioning or even socialization, we must accept all that this entails. If we can do this, then a very real source of behavioural difficulties will be removed at a stroke.

A fourth potential source of discipline troubles is removed by the change of emphasis from competition to cooperation which we have seen is implied in the introduction of a mixed-ability form of organization.

2 A. N. Whitehead, *The Aims of Education* (Macmillan, 1929), chapter 1.

Competition must generate friction and must lead to problems of behaviour in all pupils but especially in those who are not succeeding in the competitive atmosphere of the school or class. If we discourage competition, then, we remove another source of potential trouble.

At the same time, the introduction of a more cooperative approach to learning brings with it further advantages to the teacher in the matter of control and leads us on to a consideration of more positive aids to discipline that exist in the mixed-ability situation. For the move to mixed-ability classes not only removes certain factors from the teaching situation that have been productive of unsatisfactory relationships between teachers and pupils, it also introduces into the situation certain factors which, if properly used by teachers, can lead to much improved relationships. The move towards cooperation is one of these. For the mixed-ability class brings with it the notion of cooperation at all levels. Certainly the basic aim is to encourage a more collaborative approach to learning among pupils, so that relationships between pupils should be improved and the kind of friction that leads to behavioural troubles reduced. However, such an improvement in pupil–pupil relationships can only come about if there is a corresponding improvement in all relationships. We saw in chapter 3 that team-teaching with its emphasis on teachers working collaboratively with each other is an almost inevitable development from the introduction of mixed-ability classes, so that improved relationships between teachers also often follows from unstreaming. Many would also wish to bring parents more fully into the process and would wish to work for improved teacher–parent and child–parent relationships. Even if one does not go this far, there is no doubt that different pupil–teacher relationships are necessary, since a collaborative atmosphere can only be engendered if teachers collaborate with pupils as well as encouraging pupils to collaborate with each other. If this kind of improvement in teacher–pupil relationships can be brought about – and the mixed-ability class makes it possible as well as necessary – then a positive step will have been taken towards the removal of many potential discipline problems.

A second major factor in the mixed-ability class that can make a positive contribution towards improved teacher–pupil relationships and, as a result, an improved state of order within the classroom arises from this general point about collaboration. Attention has been drawn several times to the importance of creative work in the mixed-ability class and to the increased emphasis that should be placed on this kind of work. Such work both requires and contributes to differently based relationships between teachers and pupils. We can expect little creative work from pupils in a strict, authoritarian situation since this is likely to inhibit rather than promote the freedom of expression that creative work requires. A much more relaxed atmosphere is needed if pupils are to feel free to try things out. They will need to be confident that the teacher will look sympathetically on their failures as well as approvingly on their successes. Such work, then, requires teacher–pupil relationships that are based on collaboration and mutual understanding rather than on distance and control. In turn, these activities will promote this kind of teacher–pupil relationship since it will be through them that this kind of relationship based on mutual confidence will develop. There is nothing like mutual participation in a worthwhile exercise – a play, a film, a dance, a piece of music – to promote the kind of relationship we are discussing. Here, again, the mixed-ability class offers the teacher the opportunity to solve his problems of control by improving the quality of his relationships with his pupils.

One of the reasons why this kind of emphasis has been placed on the provision of opportunities for creative work in the mixed-ability class is the contribution that it can make to the emotional and social development of pupils. This concern with social and emotional development can itself be a third source of advantage to the teacher in the matter of the development of relationships with his pupils. For the teacher who is aware of his responsibility for this aspect of his pupils' development and concerned to fulfil that responsibility will quickly realize that he can only do so satisfactorily if the relationships he promotes are suitable. As we saw in chapter 4, social learning is caught rather than taught and the kind of social learning that goes on in his classroom will depend largely on the kind of relationships he is able to develop with his pupils. Again, however, at the same time as this creates a task for the teacher, it also offers him an avenue towards its achievement, since the very display of a concern with the emotional and social development of pupils will contribute to the creation of the kinds of relationship conducive to it. One cannot be genuinely concerned with a pupil's welfare without eliciting some kind of positive response from that pupil.

All of these factors, then, which are present in the mixed-ability organization create a situation in which it is easier for a teacher to develop good, productive relationships with his pupils and to avoid the worst disciplinary problems. To do so, however, he must be aware of these factors and must take advantage of the opportunities they offer. It will now be apparent, however, that the relationships they will help him to develop and, indeed, the kinds of relationship that they make essential are rather different from those that exist where a more formal approach to teaching is adopted and a more limited set of educational goals. We must now consider some of the characteristics of these new kinds of relationship.

In the first place, it will be apparent that such relationships will need to be at a very personal level. We have stressed the need for individualized learning in the mixed-ability class and for the teacher to be conscious of his responsibility for the education of thirty or more individuals rather than of one class. It will be necessary for him to get to know and understand his pupils as individuals, therefore, and this can only be done if his contact with them is a really personal one. It will also be necessary for him to make the appropriate provision for them as individuals and to cater for all aspects of their development – social and emotional as well as academic –

and this too will require personal contact with them. The class lesson, which can be a rather impersonal affair, is not the best aid to education with a mixed-ability class, so that, whether he likes it or not, the teacher cannot do his job effectively by remaining at a distance from his pupils; he must work with them, rub shoulders with them and develop relationships with them that are more personal than those that are necessary and possible in the class teaching situation.

A second, and perhaps more fundamental, feature of these new kinds of relationship is that they are the result of a concern with education in its fullest sense. If we are right to claim, as we did for example in chapter 1, that education is concerned with the development of the individual's ability to think for himself and the promotion of individual autonomy, then this cannot be promoted by authoritarian methods of control but requires the kinds of teacher–pupil relationship by which the development of the pupils autonomy, personal responsibility and independence can be assisted. I once worked with a teacher whose discipline was as tight and as authoritarian as any I have seen and who used the control he thus gained to give lessons in the workings and the advantages of the democratic way of life. Except at the rather superficial level of the purely cognitive – those boys' exercise books had to be seen to be believed – this does not work. If education implies the kind of freedom that one associates with a democratic way of life, then it will require a democratic atmosphere for its development. Reference has already been made in chapter 4 to the apparent advantages of a democratic organization for academic learning; such an organization is essential if education in the full sense is to take place. We cannot educate by coercive methods. You can drive a horse to the water, but you cannot make him drink. If you want him to drink, you must show him that it is a good thing to do so. If you want a pupil to accept the education he is offered, you must persuade him of its value. Our methods should be normative, therefore, rather than coercive, since, as we saw when discussing the value of intrinsic motivation, it is part of what it means to be educated to be brought to see the value of one's education. Nor is it enough to introduce this element in the last year or two of schooling. By then it is too late – especially for the less able. Pupils need to have experienced this kind of approach throughout their schooling, as those schools that have tried to introduce this kind of change only with their early leavers have discovered. A democratic atmosphere is essential to education at all stages and this implies teacher–pupil relationships that are in some sense democratic.

This does not mean that the teacher enters such relationships from a position of equality with his pupils or that he abandons all responsibility for the making of decisions. To say that he should not be authoritarian is not to say that he should not exercise authority; it is to say that he must look very carefully at the nature of the authority he is exercising, since its basis will be different in a democratic setting from that which it has in an overtly authoritarian one.

The teacher's authority is derived from a number of sources. He is a traditional authority figure in so far as he holds a position traditionally associated with the giving of instructions; he has the legal backing – whatever it is worth in practice – of those people and bodies who gave him his position; he should have the personal qualities necessary to secure the acceptance of his authority; and these should be associated with an expertise relevant to his job as a teacher. His authority, then, will be based both on his position and on his expertise. To put it differently, he will be *in* authority and he should also be *an* authority.

The changes that are taking place in our schools and classrooms and the changes in teacher–pupil relationships we are considering here can be summarized as the results of a move away from the positional sources of authority towards the expert, a reduction of emphasis on the teacher as *in* authority and a consequent increase of emphasis on his position as *an* authority. This reflects changes that are taking place in society as a whole, changes that are themselves the results and the overt manifestations of the move from an authoritarian to a democratic way of life. Less and less are we willing to accept authority based on position; more and more do we want to be shown that the individual has the right to exercise authority that derives from an expertise, a superior knowledge in the field concerned. It is precisely the same in the modern classroom. The teacher whose authority will be accepted is the one who makes it clear that it is based on expertise not the one who expects to be obeyed simply because he is a teacher. The new relationships to which we have been referring are those that the teacher is able to develop when his authority is accepted in this way.

There are two aspects to this expertise of the teacher, two areas in which he must be *an* authority. In the first place, he must be an authority in some field or fields of knowledge, since he must be able to meet the pupils' demands on his knowledge in the area or areas of work he is responsible for – this is one reason why team-teaching is desirable, so that the individual teacher does not have to take responsibility for more areas than he is expert in. This expertise in itself, however, will not take him far, partly because his knowledge may not be of a kind that his pupils see as worth acquiring for themselves and partly because it will in any case provide him with authority mainly in one narrow area, although there would of course be some 'spin-off' into other areas. It is for this reason that the teacher needs to be an authority in a second major sphere, that of education. He must show a professional expertise as an educator if his authority is to be accepted. It must be apparent that he knows what is best for his pupils' continued development and education and that he has the knowledge and the skills to help them to achieve it. This is the only kind of expert authority that will enable him to handle slow learners and others who are not motivated by a great desire to share his knowledge of history, physics or some other subject; it is the only kind of authority that will be accepted by pupils in their last year at school who are also usually unattracted by expertise in school subjects; it is the only kind of authority that will work in the mixed-ability class where, as we have seen, many objectives other than intellectual achievements are to be attained. It is the only kind of authority, therefore, that can provide the necessary basis for the development of the kind of teacher–pupil relationships we have described as necessary if one is to take full advantage of the opportunities the mixed-ability class offers.

To handle a class in this way, to create for oneself this kind of authority and to develop relationships with one's pupils of the kind described here is not easy. This is probably the most fundamental way in which teaching has become so much more difficult a job in recent years, although as always it has become proportionately more satisfying for the successful. It is particularly difficult for new entrants to the profession and for those nearing retirement, some of whom may feel they are too old to learn new tricks of this kind. Nevertheless, one must see this kind of change as inevitable if we are to offer pupils an education in the full sense of the word and prepare them for a free society. We must finally turn, therefore, to a consideration of some of the ways in which the teacher can achieve authority and establish relationships of this kind.

In the first place, we must stress again the improvement that follows the move to mixed-ability classes itself and the attempts to fit our educational provision to the individual.[3] As we have already said, this will not in itself solve the teacher's problem but it will create a situation in which a solution is possible and it will start him on the road to that solution. Many teachers who have experienced this have remarked on the immediate gains that are apparent once the change is effected. I have myself seen several very unpromising situations begin to offer teachers real hope of improvement once this kind of change was made. It represents, as we have said, an acceptance of all pupils and a genuine attempt to involve all equally in the life of the school. Seldom does it fail to evoke a quick response. There is a further gain when this kind of move is associated also with some form of team-teaching, since problems of control assume less significance when they are problems for the team rather than for the individual.

Of crucial importance, of course, is the attitude of the teacher or teachers involved. It is this that matters to pupils rather than the mechanics of the school organization. It is the attitude of rejection that is implicit in so much of the treatment some pupils receive at school rather than any particular method of grouping them or teaching them that creates the resentment that leads to poor relationships and behavioural troubles. A change to mixed-ability classes, or even to individual and group assignments, will not, therefore, achieve much in itself; it must be accompanied by a corresponding change in the attitudes of the teachers. Perhaps the most significant finding of the research that has been done on the relative merits of streaming and unstreaming is the clear indication that unstreaming only leads to improvements in academic attainment as well as social and

3 See B. Kaye and R. Rogers, op. cit.

emotional development when the teachers believe in it.[4] If the teacher does not believe in unstreaming, he should not teach in an unstreamed school, since he will find it difficult, if not impossible, to achieve anything there. On the other hand, if he is in sympathy with the values implicit in the change to mixed-ability classes and maintains the spirit of that change in his own teaching, then he will already have taken a major step towards the development of the kinds of relationship that are necessary. If his attitudes are appropriate, then, and those of the school as reflected in its organization are suitable, a lot will already have been achieved towards the development of the kinds of teacher–pupil relationship that we have described as necessary and the avoidance of the kinds of discipline problem that we have heard only too much about in recent years. From this point on, success or failure will depend on the individual's own qualities, his ability as a teacher, his expertise.

Clearly, in the kind of situation we are discussing the teacher's personal qualities will play a major part. The freer, more relaxed atmosphere of the classroom in which pupils are working on individual and group assignments makes more demands on the teacher's qualities as a person than the set performance at the front of a relatively homogeneous class. He needs to be able to make relationships on the basis of an easy and confident authority; he must not be heavy-handed; he must be open and friendly; and he needs a sense of humour. Relationships cannot be made from a distance nor can they be made by someone who stands too much on his dignity. It must not be thought, however, that he must be a 'born teacher'. I have never been very sure what such a creature would look like and I find it difficult to believe that anyone could be born with the sort of expertise required by a modern teacher. For, apart from the kind of personal qualities that make it possible for him to make relationships with his pupils, the teacher needs a great deal of skill and expertise of the kind that can only be acquired by hard work.

The mixed-ability class makes much greater demands on the teacher's skills and abilities as a teacher and, as we have seen, his authority will derive largely from this source. He needs as wide a knowledge as possible of the subject-matter his pupils will be working on. He also needs the specific skills that have been discussed in the earlier chapters of this book. He needs to be able to work as a member of a team; he needs to be able to group his pupils smoothly and efficiently in such a way as to avoid the behavioural problems that can arise when this is not done properly; he needs to be able to acquire or create and make available the resources that are needed by his pupils and to foresee their needs so as to have the right material to hand when he needs it and thus to avoid having pupils with nothing to do; he needs the kinds of skill necessary to care for the slow learners and non-readers and integrate them into the work of the class as a whole; in short, he needs to be an expert at his job. These skills, however cannot be acquired in isolation, as one might acquire a skill at plumbing

4 See J. C. Barker Lunn, *Streaming in the Primary School* (NFER, 1970).

joints or laying tiles. They are skills that can only be acquired and effectively employed if they are associated with a deep understanding of the nature of the educational process, the pupils we are trying to educate and the society in which the whole process takes place. An understanding of education is needed if these skills are to be used to any advantage. This indeed we have discovered in earlier chapters of this book, since it has not been possible to examine how something can be done without first establishing why we might wish to do it and the kinds of theoretical knowledge that will enable us to apply it in a given context. The teacher's professional expertise, therefore, must be seen as a number of specific skills based on as full a theoretical understanding of his task as he can acquire.

If he has this expertise, his pupils will recognize it and will respond to it. His authority will be established. He will besides have the skills necessary to avoid problems of discipline and control both with his class as a whole and with individual members of it. For these skills will enable him to organize the work of his classes with an efficiency that will forestall most problems of control. In matters of class control, prevention is not only better than cure, it is itself the only cure. For the worst cases of indiscipline cannot be cured; they can only be prevented. Prevention can only be achieved by employing the skills we have been discussing and in particular by developing the kinds of teacher–pupil relationships that we have seen are fundamental to education in the fullest sense. Control must be seen as a matter of developing relationships rather than of applying techniques.

Much can be done to provide the teacher with this kind of expertise in his initial training if this is approached in the right way. A lot must be left, however, to experience and the teacher must be so educated himself that he is able to profit from his experience, since the experience itself will teach him only what he is capable of learning from it. He must be prepared, therefore, to continue his own education by both formal and informal methods to ensure that at no stage is his professional expertise found wanting. For when it is, his control will have gone.

Chapter 8

Assessment and the Final Years of Compulsory Schooling

Changes in the provision made for the assessment of the work of pupils in secondary schools and elsewhere have been as dramatic in the last dozen years or so as any that have taken place in education. Proposals have been made, although they were subsequently rejected, for 'Q' and 'F' level examinations for the General Certificate of Education; alongside the GCE, itself only established in 1951, has been introduced the Certificate of Secondary Education; with the CSE has come a greater sensitivity to variations of approach and syllabus to be found in different schools and different parts of the country and a growing awareness of the need to devise an examination structure that could be adapted to these variations through individual assignments, assessment of course work and other new examining techniques; this has led in turn to similar adaptations in the schemes of examination of some GCE Boards[1] and recently to proposals to combine what is best in the CSE and the GCE at ordinary level into a common system of examining at 16+[2] and further proposals for the institution of a Certificate of Extended Secondary Education.

All of this activity reflects the importance of the public examination for pupils, teachers and parents. The public examination is important for pupils and parents because for them it is the key to careers of various kinds and can provide the entrée into further and higher education. It provides young people with a qualification of national currency that enables prospective employers and others to measure at least some aspects of their attainment against those of others applying for the same kind of post or further course of training or education. For teachers it is important both because it is valued by pupils and because it provides them with a clearly definable goal to work towards. Teachers want to do what is best for their pupils and they are aware that one of the ways in which they can most succeed in doing this is to help them to achieve the best qualifications they are capable of. They are also aware that the public examination can provide pupils with a source of motivation that will get them down to work and will obviate some of the behavioural difficulties associated with pupils whose sights are not fixed on this kind of external goal. Not the least important reason for the difficulties many teachers experience with classes of early leavers is the fact that they lack any incentive of this kind. We have argued elsewhere in this book the values of intrinsic motivation, of working at something because it is worth doing in itself and have offered this as a strong reason for encouraging pupils to work from their own interests,

1 See, for example, H. Macintosh, *Ideas*, no. 18, 1971 and a statement of an AEB 'O' level project in the same issue.

2 Schools Council Examinations Bulletin 23, *A Common System of Examining at 16+* (Evans/Methuen Educational, 1971).

and in chapter 7 we made out a case for solving some of our behavioural problems not by employing coercive measures but by attempting to use normative means, to show pupils the value of what we are trying to involve them in. Nevertheless, it would be hopelessly unrealistic to attempt to suggest that this is easy to achieve, or to deny that in most situations calculative measures are the ones that work and that the best way of motivating our pupils is to dangle the carrot of public achievement and future advancement before their eyes. Nor must we lose sight of the fact that, as teachers, we ourselves need some goal for our efforts and are attracted by the notion of some objective assessment of the effectiveness of our labours. Teaching offers little proof of achievement that one can put one's finger on and the public examination can compensate a little for this. For all of these reasons, then, although some teachers will claim that examinations restrict their freedom and cramp the curriculum, most will admit the key role they play in secondary education. Indeed, it was largely pressure from teachers themselves that brought about the introduction of the CSE for pupils in secondary-modern schools. I have been invited to many schools in recent years to talk to staffs about the kinds of curriculum and organizational change discussed in this book. Amid a great variety of questions put to me on these occasions, the one question that is always asked is that concerning the implications of such changes for assessment. Active concern with examining procedures stems in part, then, from the importance placed on public examinations by pupils, teachers and parents.

A second reason for the growing concern with the system of public examinations is the implications for that system of the changes that have been taking place in secondary education generally. The introduction of a statutory school-leaving age of sixteen will make the public examination more important than ever. The strongest argument for this measure is that it will enable pupils who before were forced by economic and other circumstances to leave school at fifteen to stay on to an age when they can achieve a worthwhile qualification and this will mean an increase in the number of candidates for public examinations. Teachers will also be looking to a changed provision to provide an incentive for more pupils, since many are greatly concerned about the potential behavioural problems of the extra year. The greatest source of pressure for reappraisal of the examining system, however, is the dramatic changes that are taking place in the curriculum of the secondary school and the new attitudes, approaches and methodology reflected in those changes. Recent developments in the form of examinations at both CSE and GCE ordinary level are the first attempts to bring the examining system up to date with the curriculum changes that have taken place and are taking place. New patterns of organization and new approaches to the curriculum will require new techniques of assessment and a new structure of examinations.

The introduction of mixed-ability classes, therefore, and in particular the adoption of individual and group assignment methods within these classes will have serious implications for the system of public examinations.

It may even be the case that a system of public examinations is incompatible with the individual assignment method of teaching or with the mixed-ability class, and that, whether we like it or not, we may have to give up our mixed-ability groups in the last two years of schooling and return to some form of streaming. Such a scheme has certainly been adopted by some schools where it has been felt that the present system of public examinations militates against continuing the mixed-ability form of organization beyond the third year. We must look very carefully, therefore, at the nature of examinations to discover whether they can be compatible with a mixed-ability form of grouping or whether the ideals associated with such a form of grouping must be abandoned for ever in the face of the stern realities of career prospects.

Before we do this, it may be as well to draw a distinction between internal and external examinations and to consider briefly what our approach should be to the internal assessment of the work of pupils in mixed-ability classes throughout their school careers. To do this we must be clear about the purposes of such assessments. Too often school terminal or yearly examinations are indistinguishable in either their form or their purpose from external examinations. Yet their purposes must surely be very different. For whereas the external examination has the largely administrative purpose of evaluating the level of achievement of individual pupils in national terms and awarding certificates that have a national currency and can be used anywhere in the country in the pupil's search for a job or a place in further or higher education, in short, of putting a final seal on the achievement of the pupil in his course, the internal examination must always be seen as ongoing, as diagnostic, as measuring the pupil's achievement at the present stage of a course that will continue next term or next year, so that its main purpose must be to guide the teacher in the decisions he must make concerning the individual's future education. In other words, whereas the external examination is designed mainly to provide information for outsiders – employers and the like – the internal examination's main purpose is to provide information for the teachers themselves.

If this is so, there is no reason why such internal assessments should be in any way competitive and, therefore, no reason why the need to make assessments should be seen as incompatible with the principles that underlie mixed-ability grouping. School assessment should be seen as an attempt to measure the progress of individuals in relation to their own earlier achievements rather than in competition with each other. Individual pieces of work should be assessed by comparison with other work we have had from the same pupil rather than with the work of other pupils. In some cases, that there should be any work to assess may represent a marked improvement and should be accredited accordingly. Our concern, therefore, should be not so much to give each piece of work a mark as to give the pupil the right kind of encouragement and incentive to move on to the next stage, as we suggested when discussing the correction of the work of slow learners in chapter 6, and to discover from a diagnostic viewing of the work what that next stage should be. This implies, as we have stressed throughout, playing to the strengths of pupils rather than seeking out their weaknesses. Some form of self-assessment here may be as valuable as and perhaps, from a diagnostic and motivational point of view, more valuable than the assessment made by the teacher. Progress can only really be made when the pupil himself sees the need for it and sees in detail what is involved in it. This kind of approach to internal assessment will also give the teacher greater freedom, since all pupils need not follow the same course, and will help in the development of his relationships with his pupils, since nothing can spoil such relationships more than the need to grade pupils in some kind of order of 'merit'.

At the same time, a careful record should be kept of the work of each individual so that we have an accurate account of his earlier achievements against which to assess his present work. Such an account has the advantage over the mark-book that it can include records of all aspects of the pupil's progress, his social and emotional no less than his academic development. In fact, it should be a continuing record of each individual's personal achievement and endeavour. Many teachers are now finding that in this way a profile can be built up over the full period of the pupil's course at school which is of permanent value to them and of particular value to a new teacher coming to teach him for the first time. It may also be of more value to a potential employer than some of the present public examination grades, since he might be more concerned with an applicant's ability to work with others in small group situations, to cope with occasional stresses or to stick at a problem until it is solved than with his knowledge of French irregular verbs or ability to handle the ablative absolute in Latin. In time, it might be possible to incorporate a profile of this kind in the external examination system so as to get the best of both worlds, since, as we shall see, this system still lacks the sophistication to measure many of the qualities that we are coming to regard as important. There is a need for techniques that will enable us to evaluate learning over and above the acquisition of subject-matter. We must take steps, of course, to avoid the dangers that can arise when individual teachers are asked to make this kind of subjective judgement of their pupils. The present system of record cards gives evidence of the extent to which the teacher's perception of individual pupils can be as distorted as any person's perception of another. Teachers, like anyone else, will tend to 'take to' or to 'take against' certain pupils and these initial attitudes will colour their judgement of these pupils in all contexts. Personality clashes can also occur which make any attempt at objective judgements impossible. If we are to achieve this kind of ongoing knowledge of the individual's progress, then, we shall need to employ all the techniques discussed later in this chapter, but we must remember the purposes for which we will be employing them within the school.

If the main purpose of internal assessment is to maintain this kind of continuous supervision of the progress of individuals in order to achieve greater control over that progress and more elaborate data on which we can base decisions relating to it, the main purpose of the public examination is standardization, as we have said, and this brings us to the crux of the problem. There is a need for the establishment of national standards for public examinations but there is a temptation to satisfy this need by leaving assessment to independent bodies like the Universities who, through Boards of Examiners consisting mainly of teachers, have in the past usually attempted to fulfil this function by setting common examination papers which, although carefully standardized, marked and moderated, have been able to assess only relatively limited and unsophisticated curriculum objectives and have, therefore, tended to impose a rigidity on the curriculum of the school, since teachers have naturally been tempted to limit their objectives to those that would actually be measured by the public examination. If we are to get the kind of assessment we need for the new and more sophisticated curriculum objectives we have described as the necessary corollary of mixed-ability groups, we need to look at these objectives very carefully and at the problem of assessing our success in attaining them; we need to consider some of the new techniques of assessment that have been tried in recent years to discover which are most suited to assessing our objectives; and we need to look at the extent to which teachers themselves should be involved in the assessment of their own pupils, since it would seem difficult to achieve the kind of sensitivity to the needs of individual schools and individual pupils that is needed without greater involvement of the teachers concerned. We must now look at these three aspects of the problem in some detail.

The key problem in any discussion of assessment is that of the relation of the methods of assessment to the curriculum objectives. There are very real dangers for curriculum developers here in so far as methods of assessment can govern the curriculum and, therefore, effectively inhibit curriculum development. I have seen the planning of University courses begun from a consideration of the form of examination that would be employed. That external examinations were in fact having this effect on the curriculum of the secondary school was recognized in both the Crowther[3] and Beloe[4] Reports in their discussion of external examinations for pupils who were not deemed able enough to take GCE ordinary level examinations. Both reports stressed the importance of freedom to experiment with the curriculum for these pupils; both asserted that for the most part teachers and schools were unable to influence the policy of the examinations these pupils were at that time taking; both realized that the examining bodies concerned were not in a position to keep in touch with research and development in teaching methods, although changes resulting from such research and development might require corresponding changes in examining techniques; and both felt that as a result external examinations were having the effect of inhibiting rather than promoting the kind of curriculum experimentation and development that was felt to be necessary and that

3 *15 to 18* (HMSO, 1959).
4 *Secondary School Examinations other than the GCE* (HMSO, 1960).

this was to the disadvantage not only of pupils taking these examinations but also of those not felt capable of doing so. There is no doubt that GCE ordinary level still has this kind of effect. It reflects the traditional curriculum with its emphasis on cognitive learning and its largely subject-based approach to education; it is thus based on a rather simple view of education as the acquisition of knowledge, a form of education that can be assessed more readily than most and has its attractions, therefore, both to some teachers and to examiners. As such, it provides little encouragement for curriculum development so that, not surprisingly, curriculum change has tended to begin at the other end of the scale. For, on the recommendation of the Beloe Report, a public examination was introduced, the Certificate of Secondary Education, which it was hoped would be sensitive to change and would in fact encourage teachers to experiment with curriculum provision. It must be admitted that teachers were slow at first to take advantage of the opportunities the CSE offered them to experiment with examining techniques but the movement towards this is now gaining momentum. A curriculum must be planned according to the educational needs of pupils and the educational judgement of their teachers, and techniques of assessment must be devised to fit the curriculum and adjust to it; they must not be allowed to control it. The CSE recognized this from the outset and gave teachers the opportunity to adapt the methods of assessment to their changing objectives. This they are now taking advantage of and recent developments in examining techniques can be seen as attempts to follow recent curriculum developments. It is interesting to note that some GCE Boards are now beginning to follow the lead of the CSE and are willing to experiment with new types of examination,* sometimes after direct requests from teachers but sometimes on their own initiative. Methods of assessment, therefore, must be adapted to the curriculum. New curriculum objectives require new examining techniques and changes in our curriculum objectives will require corresponding changes in our techniques of examining.

However, the changes in curriculum objectives we have discussed earlier in this book and have suggested as implied in a move to a mixed-ability form of organization are highly complex and sophisticated. There is no doubt, as we have said several times, that it is a relatively easy matter to assess the cognitive content of an individual's education, provided that we mean by this no more than the amount of information he has acquired and can recall in a given field. We have suggested that this is one reason why some teachers find this kind of somewhat limited goal attractive. We have claimed, however, that even the cognitive objectives of our curriculum should be much more sophisticated than that. To begin with, we have stressed the desirability of encouraging individual enquiries and allowing such investigations to cross the existing boundaries between subjects. The assessment of 'integrated studies' will present us with our first problems. It was also suggested earlier that education in the full sense

* See footnote 1, page 94.

cannot be assessed in terms of information acquired even in an integrated way but only in terms of the development of understanding, initiation into modes of thought, the ability to operate within and between these modes of thought, to handle the concepts appropriate to them and to think independently of authority. In short, we have provided ourselves with a set of more complex cognitive objectives which will require more sophisticated techniques of assessment than most of those now in operation if we are to measure our success in this sphere with any degree of accuracy.[5]

Furthermore, we have throughout stressed the importance of creative work in education and this will lead to even greater problems of assessment. For standards of aesthetic or artistic achievement are notoriously difficult to set and, in any case, it may not be aesthetic or artistic achievement that we are after. We may be promoting it because of its therapeutic value; we have suggested it as a device for building the confidence of slow learners; we may be using it as a means of developing the ability to enjoy and appreciate the achievements of others more expert in these fields. All of these objectives will present us with difficult problems of assessment. These are aspects of the social and emotional development of our pupils which we have also argued at some length as a prime concern of the teacher and assessment in this affective sphere will be far more difficult than in the cognitive, yet perhaps more important, if not for final external assessment, certainly for the ongoing internal assessment which is of such importance to us if we are to make the right decisions with regard to the educational progress of individual pupils.

Most of these affective objectives are of such a long-term nature as to make it difficult for any one teacher to evaluate his own achievements in this area with his pupils, except in the unlikely event of his having charge of them for most of their school careers. This suggests the need for a plan of evaluation at the school level, involving all of the teachers concerned with each individual. The complexities of such a plan will be apparent. We must also remember that cognitive and affective objectives can for the most part be distinguished only at the conceptual level. In practice, they will inevitably be interwoven. It is not possible to distinguish learning to enjoy physics from the acquisition of certain cognitive abilities connected with that subject or to speak of the development of an interest in something without assuming at the same time the acquisition of some knowledge in that area; nor, conversely, is it possible at any but an extremely superficial level to acquire knowledge in a field without any kind of motivation towards it. The complexities of these objectives and the interrelationships between them make the assessment of their achievement a highly complex matter and highlight the need for continuing research in this field and for the employment of more sophisticated techniques of examining.

It has become increasingly clear in recent years that the essay-type question, once a regular feature of almost all examination papers, has

5 See B. S. Bloom (ed.), *Taxonomy of Educational Objectives*, vol. 2 (Longman, 1964), especially chapters 2 and 6.

serious drawbacks to it for most kinds of assessment and slowly it is being replaced or supplemented by other methods. It is clearly not very helpful in the assessment of the kinds of objective we have just listed. It also has serious disadvantages even when it comes to the assessment of purely cognitive achievements. To begin with, it is open to inconsistencies of marking both between different members of an examining board and even within the marking of an individual examiner. There has always been some point to the hope expressed by most of us at some time that the examiner would settle down to read a particular offering of ours only after he had enjoyed a good dinner. Furthermore, there are serious difficulties in achieving comparability of assessment between candidates. Most papers of this kind offer a range of questions from which each candidate must choose three or four. This gives a very uneven sampling of the field supposedly covered, opens the system up to the inaccurate results that arise from successful or unsuccessful question 'spotting' by candidates and, in particular, raises the problem of how we can achieve comparability of assessment between the candidate who chooses to write, say, a largely factual account of Caesar's conquest of Gaul and the one who chooses to wrestle with the complex political events leading to his crossing the Rubicon. Such examinations do test the candidate's ability to marshal his material, to select what is relevant and to develop a coherent argument, but these abilities can perhaps be tested just as well by other methods, by timed essays and open-book examinations and the factual content perhaps more accurately by objective tests.

The timed essay and the open-book examination can be regarded as variations on a similar theme, since both of them allow the examinee access to research and resource material after he knows the questions the examiners are setting him. Either he is given the questions in advance and allowed to prepare beforehand to write an essay in a given time or he is allowed to bring books and other material with him into the examination. In both cases, it is assumed that the examiner will thus gain a clear impression of the candidate's ability to seek out and select information relevant to his subject and to deploy it effectively and quickly.

The individual's grasp of the factual material itself can be assessed by the use of objective tests and this is becoming an increasingly popular way of testing for knowledge of basic information. Objective questions at any level of sophistication are difficult to set but they are very easy to mark. They can be marked by clerks or even by machines, since on each question the candidate is asked to select from a number of possible answers and there can only be one right answer to each question. Thus they score very highly on marker reliability,[6] since there is no room for the subjective judgement of the marker, and they can cover much more of any syllabus than the essay paper, since without the need for essay writing a candidate can answer a large number of questions on any one paper. For the testing of information acquired, then, such tests have much to recommend them

6 See M. Connaughton, *Educational Research*, 1969.

and they would seem to do this job better than those asking essay-type questions. They are also relatively easy to administer and this may be an important consideration if the number of pupils to be assessed rises as it is expected to. Since they do test only information acquired, however, we must not let their other attractive features tempt us into adopting them to the exclusion of other forms of assessment.

A completely different approach to assessment, but one which has become increasingly popular in recent years, is to base evaluation not on the pupil's performance in tests or papers undertaken at certain set times and under certain prescribed conditions, or not solely on this kind of information, but on the work done by the pupil throughout his course. This may take several forms. It may be based on the written work that he is required to do from time to time during his course; it may be that his teacher or teachers will be asked to make an assessment based on their view of his work over the full period of the course; or he may be asked to submit a special exercise, a project of some kind on an area he has selected to study. This seems to offer some hope of being able to make an assessment of the complex objectives we discussed earlier and also of being able to preserve some of the individual and group assignment work and enquiry- and interest-based approaches to teaching we have emphasized earlier. It can only be done, however, if teachers are more fully involved in the public assessment procedures, since their contribution is required either in the advice they must give to pupils on the selection of subjects for study or in the actual evaluation of their work. We must now consider, therefore, the whole question of the involvement of teachers in public assessments.

The CSE was planned from the outset in such a way as to give teachers control over it and this was done in order to prevent it from having the kind of inhibiting effect on curriculum development that we referred to earlier. Schools have been allowed to choose from three modes of examining for each subject the one they felt to be best suited to them. Under Mode 1, candidates sit examination papers on syllabuses set and published by a Regional Board. There are fourteen such boards in England and Wales and in each region syllabuses are designed and papers set and marked by bodies consisting mainly of local teachers. Mode 2 allows for the planning of syllabuses by individual schools or groups of schools, subject to the general approval of the Regional Board, but requires that pupils take external examinations on these syllabuses. A school opting for Mode 3 can set and mark its own examinations or individual assignments, subject only to moderation by the Regional Board. Initially, Mode 1 attracted most support, but Mode 3 has been attracting the increasing interest of teachers in recent years. A feature of the CSE from the beginning in all three modes has been the extent to which new techniques of assessment have been employed. Course work assessment, objective testing, project work and oral examining have all been used in an attempt to devise more and more subtle devices for assessing the teachers' increasingly complex objectives. There are two aspects of this which are worthy of comment.

In the first place, it would seem that the intention of the planners to ensure that CSE did not come to have an inhibiting effect on the development of new curriculum objectives has been fulfilled. If we want to encourage teachers to experiment with the curriculum and to try new approaches, we must give them effective control of the techniques and procedures of assessment so that they can feel free to try things out without jeopardizing the chances of their pupils to attain qualifications and, as a result, their career prospects. It is also important to make it possible to develop the curriculum and the techniques of assessment together, since they are closely interlinked. The claim that teachers should have a major responsibility for assessment procedures would appear vindicated by the experiences of the CSE. To yield control of assessment to outside bodies is to yield control of the curriculum. There must be real contact between teachers and examiners, between those who plan and operate the curriculum and those who have the expertise in techniques of assessment, and, where curriculum development is going on in a formal way, the curriculum developers must be brought in too. But if the teacher is to have the sort of freedom we have argued for to make the kinds of educational decision we have said are necessary in the individualized learning situation of the mixed-ability class, he must be confident that he can ensure that the assessment techniques will assess what he is doing and not what some outside body feels he ought to be doing.

The second aspect of this involvement of teachers in the assessment of their pupils that we must look at carefully is their responsibility in some cases for actually assessing their own pupils' work. There is some evidence to suggest* that such assessments are at least as valid as those achieved by other means and possibly more so, since, being spread over a long period of time, such assessment avoids many of the difficulties such as illness or 'nerves' of the single occasion examination. However, the need to make these assessments does raise a number of problems. It can make heavy demands of teachers, who are likely to be already busy enough, since it will be necessary for them, if they are to do this job properly, to agree on standards, to devise appropriate tests and other forms of assessment and to attend to whatever moderation procedures are deemed necessary. It can create difficulties too in the very tender and sensitive area of teacher–pupil relationships which we have already discussed at some length. It does not require much imagination to realize how such relationships can be jeopardized when the teacher assumes the role of examiner, concerned no longer to advise and encourage but to assess and grade. For this reason, among others, it is difficult, if not impossible, for the individual teacher to achieve complete objectivity and impartiality in his assessment of his own pupils. We must also remember the need for standardization between schools and teachers in an assessment of this kind, since these certificates must have a valid national currency.

Most of these difficulties can be overcome, however, if an adequate

* See footnote 6, page 101.

system of moderation can be devised. Such a system will protect the teacher from the final responsibility and the fear of being influenced by either a 'halo' effect or whatever its opposite is – presumably a 'forked tail' effect; it will also protect the pupil and it should safeguard teacher–pupil relationships. There are a number of methods by which moderation of this kind can be achieved. In some cases teachers work in groups within a school or between several schools and check each other's assessments by sampling the work of each other's pupils. Sometimes visits are made to schools by moderators from Regional Boards to sample the work of pupils and to check the standards of assessment being used against those they have experienced in other schools. A third method is to set a common paper to candidates from all schools. The results of this test may or may not count towards the final grade, but in either case it acts as a check on the individual teacher's assessment. Combinations of these methods and other more sophisticated methods of moderation are being tried and it is not impossible, therefore, to ensure that the involvement of teachers in assessment need not result in a loss of standardization of grading or of the value of such awards as national currency.

If we accept that it is possible to avoid these difficulties, then, the use of teachers' assessments in the overall grading of pupils is of enormous advantage. It provides us with a real chance of finding a method of assessing those complex objectives we discussed earlier. Mode 3 of the CSE has begun to reveal techniques of assessment that hold out real hope for the future and it is not surprising to discover some GCE ordinary level Boards beginning to follow the lead thus given.* Continuous assessments of various kinds, project work of the kind associated with CSE Mode 3 and many forms of test and written examination provide us with a range of techniques from which we might hope to find combinations to evaluate quite sophisticated curriculum objectives in a way that will preserve national standards. Furthermore, if teachers are involved at all levels in the processes of assessment and feel that they are in control of it, this can be achieved without the imposition of rigidity on the curriculum of the secondary school and without inhibiting curriculum development. The freedom of both teachers and pupils can be maintained.

A great deal of research and development is, of course, needed in this area and here again teachers need to be trained in the necessary skills if they are to play this kind of major part in the final assessment of their pupils, but this is the direction in which things seem to be going. In this context, it comes as no surprise to find proposals being put forward by a Working Party set up by the Schools Council for a common system of examining at 16+.† Such a system is proposed to replace both CSE and GCE ordinary level examinations. It would hope to deal with the increased number of candidates expected as a result of the raising of the school-leaving age to sixteen and with the wider range of abilities that this will also bring. It is suggested that it should be controlled by the teachers on

* See footnote 1, page 94.   † See footnote 2, page 94.

a regional basis so as to ensure teacher control of the curriculum. It would aim to employ a number of techniques of examining, methods of assessment and moderating procedures. Like the CSE, it would seek to grade pupils but would not use the categories of pass or fail. It would thus attempt by as many means as possible to provide pupils with a leaving certificate which did in fact give potential employers and others as much valid information as it was possible to obtain.

If we have this kind of assessment, largely teacher controlled and with scope for CSE Mode 3 techniques, there is more freedom for the individual teacher and, therefore, more scope for the individual or group assignment and for interest-based and enquiry-based approaches to teaching. These methods of learning, which we have regarded as an essential part of the mixed-ability class, can be maintained until the end of the fifth year without threat to national standards or jeopardy to the qualifications and career prospects of the pupils. It is still not clear, however, whether the mixed-ability class itself can survive into the final year of compulsory schooling. The proposals for a common 16+ examination envisage provision only for the percentile range 40–100, the top 60 per cent of each age group, and although, as the report of the Working Party points out, some pupils below this range may be able to take the examination in some subjects and school-based syllabuses may cater for others, this will still leave a large number of pupils with no public assessment to work towards in their final years of schooling.

Most teachers nowadays would agree that it is not necessary to start pupils on the present CSE and GCE ordinary level syllabuses in most subjects until two years, three at the most, before the examination. There is little threat to mixed-ability classes, once established, therefore, in the first three years of the secondary school. The crucial question is how far they can be continued after that, how far it is possible to prepare pupils for examinations in mixed-ability classes alongside the large number of pupils who have no such goal or incentive. It is sometimes claimed that CSE Mode 3 can provide the answer here and can extend the freedom of schools and teachers to maintain their mixed-ability classes to the end. On the other hand, while this may have been possible in some schools when a large proportion of the less able left at fifteen, giving the others a clear run of at least one year to their external examinations, it must become more difficult now that they are all required by law to remain until the end. Many schools have already found it impossible to keep their mixed-ability classes beyond the second or third year and have, therefore, reverted to some form of streaming in the upper school. It has sometimes been argued that streaming can be 'natural' at this stage, that it can be a kind of 'self-streaming', since it is based on greater evidence of the individual's abilities than has been available before and on the realistic choice of the individual of the kind of course he would like to follow with his future career in mind. However, we have argued strongly earlier in this book the case for mixed-ability classes on the grounds of their contribution to the social and emotional development of all pupils, both the able and the less able; we have discussed the advantages of this form of grouping for the development of the kinds of relationship between teachers and pupils that education in its fullest sense seems to require; and we have stressed the importance of avoiding the behavioural problems that result from gathering all the less able pupils into a 'ghetto' class and labelling them as failures. If these arguments have any validity in the educational provision for younger children, they must have at least equal validity when we come to consider that of older pupils. Indeed, we know that the older the pupils the more difficult they are to handle in this kind of situation. We should be reluctant, therefore, to break up the social groupings that have existed earlier in the school and to throw away the advantages we can hope to have gained from two or three years of mixed-ability groupings. As we have said before, we can only hope to achieve the complex objectives we have set ourselves if the whole educational environment, including our administrative procedures, are geared towards the achievement of them. We must finally turn, then, to a consideration of how these groupings might be maintained in the final years of compulsory schooling.

In doing so, it might be as well to begin from a consideration of some of the things those pupils whose general ability does not seem to warrant their taking external examinations should be doing in the last years at school. As a general principle, they should be engaged in activities that they can themselves see as having value for them. If they are not to become a threat to the good order of the school, they will need to be kept occupied and, for all the reasons we gave in chapter 7, they can only be kept properly occupied if they can be persuaded to accept the value of what they are doing or can be allowed to do the things they regard as valuable. This is one good reason for continuing to allow them to work through their interests and on their own individual or group enquiries. We shall not get far if we take the attitude of the teacher I once heard complaining, 'I can't teach these fourth years any physics. All they are interested in is motor-bikes.' A lot can still be done to promote their education through the interests they reveal and this should continue. As a young teacher, I myself succeeded, more by luck perhaps than judgement, in turning a difficult class of leavers into a collection of purposeful and interested workers by ignoring the syllabus I had been given and inviting them to take on an individual project within the subject area I was responsible for, namely geography. I got work from those boys that I had not thought they were capable of and life became much more pleasant for them and for me.

In addition to the continuation of this kind of provision, however, there are certain specific things that they all become interested in during the years preceding their final departure from school. In particular, they become interested in their future work and all that is associated with it. There is no doubting, therefore, the need for their curriculum to contain a large vocational component at this stage. There are at least three elements in this provision. They need to be provided, where this is possible, with the beginnings of some of the specific skills they may need in the job they will enter; they need a more general introduction to the world of work, to the basic features of working life; and they need extensive guidance in their choice of a career.

In most situations it may not be possible for the school to do a lot to provide pupils with specific industrial skills. In many cases they may be going into too many quite different careers for this even to be considered. Where there is a dominant local industry, however, to which most of them will go, it would seem only good sense to give them whatever help the school can give in preparation for this. Obviously, the workshop staff have a major contribution to make here and it is always noticeable how seldom disciplinary problems arise when boys of this age are engaged in the kinds of activity that modern handicraft teachers can involve them in. With girls the domestic science staff will be similarly involved and, we hope, to the same effect. We should be wary nowadays, however, of being too ready to allocate sex roles in this way. Unisex is as much a feature of education as of society as a whole and schools are producing as many male cooks as expert craftswomen. Schools should do whatever they can, in the light of local conditions, to help pupils in this way. Linked courses with Colleges of Further Education can be particularly valuable here since they can enable pupils to get the kind of vocational course most schools are not equipped to provide, they can bring to the pupil's attention the range of post-school education that is available and they can enable him to spend some of his time in a situation where he can have more personal responsibility.

Much more important, however, is the provision of courses of preparation for the world of work. This is something all pupils need and if the school does not provide them with it no one will. It is a major step to move from the relatively cloistered atmosphere of even a large modern comprehensive school to a factory, a shop, an office or a typing pool and this is an experience few teachers have had, since transition from school to work for them was cushioned by a period of time at college or university. To begin with, one is in school as of right; one is at work only if one can show that one has a contribution to make. The school is, for the most part, a society of young people; at work there will be people of all ages, from sixteen to sixty-five. There is often an abrupt change of values, of attitudes and of atmosphere. On top of that there are things like income tax, insurance contributions, benefits, pension schemes, unions and a hundred other new things to cope with. This is a transition that cannot be made smoothly unless the school helps pupils to make it. This means that they must be provided with a lot of basic information about conditions of employment and the like and must be prepared in every way possible for the new situation they are about to enter. Some schools have experimented with the simulation of work conditions in the school. They have required the older pupils to 'clock' in and out and have introduced production or bonus-incentive schemes into their work. The 'spin-off' advantages of this kind of approach are not to be scorned too readily by teachers concerned to motivate pupils in their final years at school. Another way of preparing pupils for work is to arrange for them to visit places of work in the locality. Such visits should, if possible, not be merely guided tours conducted by the manager; there should be an opportunity for them to mix with and talk to the men and women on the shop floor and to find out at first hand what it is really like to work there. If it can be arranged for them to visit such places on a more regular basis and perhaps actually work in them for part of the week, this will be even more advantageous, since a phased transition from school to work then becomes possible with school support and supervision of the intermediate phase. Such a course may be extended to or developed from a wider course of education for citizenship – certainly there is much to be said for attempting to put all of this into a broader context – but the important thing is that the school should accept and face up to its responsibility in this area.

As a part of such a course and as an integral part of the provision made by a school for its pupils, guidance in the matter of choosing a suitable career is of absolutely vital importance. Stories of boys and girls going through a dozen or more jobs in the first months after leaving school are not uncommon nor are they particularly surprising when one considers the inadequacy of the provision made for advice on these matters by many schools. This must be a major concern of the pupil in his final year, if not before, and we cannot really expect to win his respect or his attention if we do not take it very seriously. To take it seriously involves a lot. It is important, first of all, to provide information about the jobs that are available, the career prospects that they offer, the conditions of work and the qualifications needed for them. Such information can be provided by pamphlets, by visits from representatives of the firms and sometimes by films and other publicity material of this kind. All of these facilities should be made available to the greatest extent possible. To provide all of this is only to scratch the surface of the problem, however, since none of it will help the pupil to discover what it is like to work in this factory or that office nor to know whether he is suited to that particular kind of work. Provision of information needs to be supplemented by the kind of visit to local places of employment we have just described and, if possible, opportunities to try working in them to get the feel of them.

None of this will be of full value, however, if the pupil is not given all of the help he can be given with the task of discovering the kind of job he is personally suited for. It is not enough to ask a pupil in his last year or his last term what he wants to do or to push him towards that which he is qualified to do. Dissatisfaction arises when a young person finds himself in a job that may have appeared attractive but which he quickly finds is not his thing. If pupils are to be helped with this and given appropriate advice, then teachers need a great deal of data about them as individuals. This is another way in which the profile can be of great value, but it must be a profile drawn up with this as one of its specific concerns, since it must include the results of aptitude and interest tests, not necessarily highly sophisticated, that have been used over a period of time to build up a picture of each pupil's aptitudes, interests and preferences as well as his capabilities. Without this sort of data it is sheer arrogance to assume that careers advice can be given, but such advice must be given and it must be readily available.

Nor can this be left until the last few weeks or the last term before the pupil leaves school, when the Youth Employment Officer calls to give each pupil an interview that the magnitude of his task makes necessarily brief. Advice and information should be available and should be given throughout the last two years of schooling at least. Some would wish to begin much earlier than this and start children thinking about these issues almost from the outset of their secondary-school careers. Certainly, the matter of building up an aptitude and interest profile cannot be begun too soon and it is most desirable that formal arrangements be made for careers 'lessons' throughout the secondary-school course. If this is to be done properly, again it will place a heavy burden on teachers. In this field, however, it is relatively easy to delegate prime responsibility to a specialist careers master or mistress. This does not mean that the other teachers can forget their responsibilities here, but it does mean that much of the hard work, collecting information, testing for aptitudes, arranging visits and so on can be done by one man or woman with a time-table and other provision to enable him or her to do it thoroughly. It also means that all pupils can benefit from the advice of a member of staff who himself has had industrial experience, since first-hand experience of this kind would seem to be an essential qualification for such a post.

The whole area of vocational preparation, then, is a huge one and one that must loom very large in the final years of compulsory schooling. A second area of great importance is that of community service.[7] We have already referred to this in stressing the need of slow learners in particular to feel wanted and needed and to be shown ways in which they can make a valuable contribution to their community. Many schools have found this a valuable and important element in the education of their fifteen- and sixteen-year-olds. It can give them a sense of purpose that will obviate some of the behavioural problems that can arise at this age; it contributes also to their social education in that through it they can learn to care for others, and to put themselves into the position of others; thus they learn something about the interdependence of men. It can also be developed into a course of some substance at the cognitive level since active involvement in community service can act as a basis for a social studies course that may be more worthwhile than many such courses that are being offered at present.

Indeed, this interest in community service must be seen as one aspect of the interest that is shown by all pupils at this stage of their development

7 See Schools Council Working Paper no. 17, *Community Service and the Curriculum* (HMSO, 1968).

in the world outside their own immediate environment of school and home. It is at this time that their attention turns outwards and they become interested in social issues, in national and world problems, in political and moral questions. It is at this time too that they are most in need of moral guidance, since developing sexual maturity and the approach of adult status bring feelings of independence and personal moral problems for which personal solutions must be found. They can no longer be buttressed from such issues by their parents; they must face them themselves. The guidance they need, therefore, cannot take the form of moral precepts; they must be given opportunities for and help with informed discussion of these issues if they are to be able to reach sound and considered conclusions on them, at least on those that affect their own lives and behaviour. It is the aim of the Schools Council Humanities Curriculum Project, to which we have already referred several times, to help teachers to give their pupils this kind of opportunity and to provide them with some of the resources needed if they are to do so. Other material is also available to teachers who wish to help their pupils with this kind of exploration.[8] Again, it is an area which, because of its importance to the pupils, teachers cannot afford to ignore.

All of these elements in the work of the final years of schooling can be developed into viable courses and even into courses leading to publicly approved qualifications. They should not be seen as necessarily something that is done to 'keep them off the streets' or to provide them only with the very practical help they need. All are very important elements in the education of these young people and can provide a basis for worthwhile courses leading, particularly via Mode 3 techniques, to recognizable qualifications for pupils who might otherwise have been regarded as 'unexaminable'. It is not necessary to see the public examination as concerned only with traditional academic subjects. Anything we regard as being educationally important we should be prepared to recognize and to offer pupils qualifications for if they reach a level of attainment that warrants it. If we take this view, it becomes possible to find areas in which public qualifications are within reach of a great many more of our pupils than appear able to achieve them at present and thus to provide them with a valuable source of motivation for their efforts during their final year. An increasing number of schools are finding it possible to devise courses which lead to CSE qualifications – with parallel GCE ordinary level courses in some cases too – but which, being based on individual assignment and enquiry methods, provide scope for a wider range of children than would normally be expected to reach this kind of level. Where parallel CSE and GCE courses have been made available, candidates have been entered for one or the other examination according to their level of achievement.[9] Humanities courses and other courses of 'integrated studies'

8 See, for example, *Connexions* (Penguin).
9 For an account of one such experiment see A. Gregson and W. Quin, *Dialogue*, Schools Council Newsletter no. 10, 1972.

seem to offer particular opportunities here and the next stage of this process is the designing of syllabuses to be submitted to both CSE and GCE boards. Such a syllabus has, for example, been devised and submitted by the staff of Conisbrough Northcliffe County High School. Described in the submission as 'not a watered down GCE syllabus for submission to the CSE Board, but a genuine syllabus which puts the future educational needs of the children before every other consideration', it is a course of integrated studies on a series of topics influenced by and based loosely on the Schools Council Humanities Curriculum Project, and so planned as to encourage a degree of individual pupil choice within a broad framework of common ground and to allow grades to be separately determined for the four subjects principally involved in the project, English, Geography, History and Religious Education. Evaluation is to be based on the continuous assessment of course work and a final dissertation. Such a scheme points conclusively to the need for a common system of examining at 16+; it also draws attention to opportunities that the mixed-ability class can provide for teachers who are prepared to approach the education of their less able pupils with imagination and confidence. The 'self-fulfilling prophecy' can work to raise the level of pupils' achievement as well as to lower it and pupils of all abilities can continue to work together throughout their school careers.

Furthermore, in listing earlier the provision that needs to be made for less able pupils, we touched on nothing that is of any less value to those who are to take public examinations and even to stay on for advanced courses. He would be a brave man who would claim that such pupils do not need opportunities to discuss moral issues, the social education that comes from community service or the confidence and security that can come from proper vocational guidance. Indeed, it is often claimed that university entrants and university graduates show the lack of proper vocational guidance more than most, since they have so often not been advised on the subjects to study or the courses to take with particular careers in view. It may be that in the fourth and fifth years these pupils need a differently balanced diet from that of their fellows who will leave at sixteen, but it is hard to say that they need a totally different kind of provision.

If we add to these points the advantages we claimed earlier for the mixed-ability class, particularly the behavioural advantages, since it is this that worries teachers more than anything else, we can see that together they constitute a strong argument for continuing this kind of organization throughout the school. There is a great deal of work that all pupils can undertake in common even at this stage in education and there is great value still in the sharing of experiences. There is still a place for individual assignments and for group work and, while this is so, there is no reason to abandon our mixed-ability groupings. Given the kind of flexible timetable suggested in chapter 2, we can allow time for this kind of work, while making equal provision for the specific needs of different groups –

ordinary level physics, brick-laying courses at the local technical college, vocational guidance, housecraft – at other times. We have already suggested that, on the basis of mixed-ability classes, the timetable should allow for remedial work for all and perhaps also for the teaching of certain subjects; we are now suggesting that it might also allow for special courses of many kinds.

Unless we can retain the mixed-ability class to the end, we will create classes of leavers that will be a constant source of disruption to the life of the school and the extra year will become the hazard to life and limb that many teachers expect it to be. Nor will we have attained anything of value if our mixed-ability groupings are abandoned after three or four years. For with them we will have abandoned our values and our ideals and the pupils will see them for the empty things they are. We need to be consistent in our attitudes; we need to see secondary education, and indeed all education, as a continuous process with the same basic principles throughout. Just as we must not allow external assessment to rule our objectives, so we must not allow it to govern the administrative procedures we adopt to achieve them, since, as we have seen, these procedures themselves have an educative function and, if our objectives are to be achieved to any extent, the whole educational environment must be directed towards their achievement.

Chapter 9

The Education of Teachers

The earlier chapters of this book have attempted to deal with some of the many complexities of teaching in a school that organizes its pupils into mixed-ability classes and it will be clear to anyone who has struggled through them that teaching in all schools is now a much more complicated and highly skilled business for all teachers than it once was. It is not enough now, therefore, to give every intending secondary teacher a 'methods' course in the teaching of his own subject, no matter how elaborate such a course may be. He needs an expertise in so many other fields as well, as the earlier chapters of this book have indicated, and, as we have also seen, his authority and control will largely depend on the extent to which he achieves a mastery of these skills.

It is important too to remember that student teachers are entitled to an education as well as a training. When the Robbins Report[1] recommended that Training Colleges be restyled Colleges of Education, it was endeavouring to underline by this change of nomenclature the new role that these institutions had come to have or should come to have as a branch of higher education concerned with the personal education of their students as well as their preparation for a particular career. It was also reflecting the growing awareness that, even when the matter is viewed from an entirely professional point of view, intending teachers must be educated rather than trained. For it is no longer possible to regard these objectives as separate or to accept the validity of such a dichotomy. A successful teacher will need not only the skills we have referred to but also the kind of theoretical understanding of education that will enable him to use them in a professional manner in his teaching. No teacher can do his job properly without this understanding and, therefore, no teacher can be regarded as professionally qualified unless his preparation has gone considerably beyond that which can be dubbed 'training'.

Our concern, then, must be with the education of teachers and we must approach the planning of all elements of the course with this in view. All of these elements will also need to be interrelated, but it may be helpful to distinguish them here in order to make clear what is or should be involved in each. These basic elements would seem to be four in number – the student's own area or areas of learning, usually known as his 'main subject', his theoretical understanding of education, his practical or professional studies and his practical work in schools. In the case of graduates, it will normally be assumed that the first of these will have been dealt with during their degree courses; in the case of students on concurrent courses all four elements will normally be going on side by side. We must now

1 *Higher Education* (HMSO, 1963).

look at these four areas in turn to see what each should contribute to the total education of the kind of teacher that we have suggested the mixed-ability class and the school of the near future will need.

The main subject, more obviously than any other element in the student teacher's course, has the dual role of contributing to the student's own further education and providing him, particularly if he is preparing to teach in secondary schools, with a teaching subject.[2] It would be difficult to decide which of these two objectives is the more important. Certainly, there is little point in providing potential secondary teachers with a course that is so esoteric as to have little relevance in the classroom; but it is equally unsatisfactory to expect a teacher to take responsibility for the education of others if he has not had an education in the full sense himself. Nor need it be assumed that a concern with the professional relevance of the main subject must result in a reduction of the intellectual rigour demanded by the study. Indeed, it may be argued that such a concern should rather lead to increased intellectual demands since a desire to prepare oneself to educate others may lead to a higher level of motivation and the teaching of a subject will always make greater demands of the intellect than the learning of it. Main courses must be planned with both of these requirements in mind.

If the main course is to meet both these needs, we must look very carefully at the content of all such main courses. In this connection, it is perhaps worth noting the unsuitability for potential teachers of some existing degree courses, which being designed for all-comers clearly cannot be tailored to the needs of intending teachers. This difficulty has been resolved in some places by the development of concurrent courses leading to a first degree and to a teaching qualification at the same time. This kind of course, apart from sharing the other advantages of concurrent training, makes it possible to adapt the content of the degree course to the needs of intending teachers and thus to attempt to achieve both the objectives we have been discussing.

The key problem here is the question of whether it is best for the student, as a student and as an intending teacher, to study one area in depth, as he is at present required to do in most degree courses and a majority of main courses in Colleges of Education, or to cover a number of areas in breadth, as was suggested by the James Report[3] on the training of teachers. Opinions are divided here, but there are a number of factors to keep in mind when attempting to reach a conclusion on this issue.

In the first place, we must remember that it is not necessary to continue to think in terms only of traditional subject areas. Many colleges have in recent years been moving into other fields of study, as indeed have some universities. Courses in such things as American Studies, Language Studies, Film and Television, Creative Arts and other similar areas have begun to appear in the prospectuses of many colleges and courses of this kind

2 See S. Hewett (ed.), *The Training of Teachers* (ULP, 1971), pp. 84 ff.
3 *Teacher Education and Training* (HMSO, 1972).

may, if properly planned and conducted, offer the advantages of both breadth and depth of study, as well as providing the intending teacher with the kind of first-hand experience of integrated studies that might help him to contribute to this kind of course in a school.

There is little evidence of the relative educational merits of breadth and depth of study, but it is important that we do not try to make our potential secondary teachers take too many subjects. If we do, they will inevitably not become expert in any of them and, therefore, will be in no position to provide their pupils with an education of any real merit. In concerning ourselves with the less able pupils in the mixed-ability class, we must not lose sight of the fact that the future graduates will also be there, and that they will need teachers who have real expertise in certain subject areas. Indeed, as we said in chapter 7, they are likely only to accept the authority of those teachers who show such expertise. The mixed-ability class is no place for the 'general teacher'. It was for this reason among others that we suggested that some form of team-teaching is an inevitable development of the individual assignment work associated with mixed-ability classes.

Team-teaching, as we said in chapter 3, enables pupils to have the advice of experts in all fields and obviates the need to try to give teachers a smattering of knowledge in a great many areas. However, team-teaching, and indeed any form of integrated studies programme, also requires that each member of the team, although a specialist, should have an awareness of and a sympathy towards other areas of work. Our main courses, then, while not being superficial, should aim to give students this kind of perspective and to give them a competence in one or two subjects without making them subject bound. This can probably only be done if there is considerable collaboration between specialist subject tutors.

Provided that we bear these points in mind, there is probably a place for both kinds of course, both the narrower kind of study in depth and the broader courses that are now being suggested. The important thing is that the provision should be flexible enough to allow for the different learning styles of students, since there is no one way of educating teachers any more than there is one way of educating pupils in school.

The most maligned element in initial courses for teachers has always been the theoretical study of Education. Teachers, as well as students, have been individually and collectively critical of the 'over-theoretical' nature of some courses of training and have demanded that they be made more practical. The James Report took a similar line and suggested that much of the theoretical study of Education could be left until later when some teachers may feel the need of it. While it is no doubt true that in many cases such studies have tended to be too remote from the realities of the school and the classroom situation and have been somewhat inclined to require that students become philosophers, psychologists, sociologists or even all three rather than educationists, it is surely not true that teachers do not need any theoretical understanding of their professional concerns beyond that which will contribute to the skills they need in the classroom nor is it true that these skills can be acquired and practised without any kind of theoretical underpinning.

One of the things that distinguishes the professional man from the tradesman is his understanding of the total context in which his own particular professional duties are carried out. One expects a doctor to be competent to give a professional opinion on any medical matter and to be able to contribute to discussions of major principles of medical provision, not merely to be able to mend bones and cure ailments. In education, decisions of that kind are perhaps more important since they need to be taken more often; for education, by its very nature, cannot have the relatively clear goals and objectives that medicine for the most part has. Decisions of this kind in education, then, if not taken by teachers themselves, will be taken for them by others, by politicians and administrators. The teacher who demands that he be troubled with only that theoretical study which has direct relevance for his own classroom is tacitly demanding that he be absolved of the responsibility for the more far-reaching decisions that constantly need to be made and that someone else make these decisions for him. It is hardly a professional attitude that such a teacher is adopting.

Furthermore, as we argued earlier, it is doubtful if this is a tenable position to adopt, since even the immediate problems of the classroom require of the teacher a deep theoretical understanding of education. This book is in itself proof of this, since it has not been possible in it to tell teachers how to group their pupils, how to teach their slow learners, how to develop the kinds of teacher–pupil relationship that will lead to good behaviour and satisfactory social and emotional development, but only to attempt to provide them with the kind of general understanding of the issues involved that will enable them to make their own decisions in the highly individual context of their own schools and classrooms. Teachers must be educated to understand the job they are doing so that they can see for themselves how these things apply to their own work. They need a wide range of skills but, more importantly, they need the understanding to apply these skills to their own teaching. The teacher needs to be exercising his professional judgement all the time – particularly if he has a mixed-ability class and is working through individual and group assignments. Unlike the plumber, or even the doctor, he is faced not only with problems of means but daily with searching questions concerning ends and aims. To do his own job in his own classroom satisfactorily, therefore, he needs an understanding of education in the fullest sense. Only thus will he be able to develop his own individual style of teaching and only thus will he be able to do a professional job. Without this theoretical underpinning, there can be no practical training that is of any value.

To be able to do a proper professional job in the classroom and to be able to contribute to the educational debate in the way that every teacher should be able to contribute, a deep involvement in the theoretical study of education is necessary. This must include a knowledge of the physical development of children and the kind of insight into their psychological development, their mental processes and the interrelationships between them and others that psychology can offer; it must embrace an understanding of the society in which the children live and will continue to live and of the many social groups they belong to, including those within the school; it must involve the kind of understanding of the contemporary educational scene that can only come from an examination of its organizational structure and its historical origins; and it must take in also a consideration of other societies, whether similar to or different from our own, since there is much to learn from looking at other people's problems and at the solutions they have discovered for them. There must also be careful consideration of theories of education, of attempts to state what education should be aiming to do, and detailed analysis of the language in which all educational assertions are expressed in order to ensure clarity of thinking in educational debate. All of these are, of course, interrelated and we must beware of encouraging the student to become too involved in particular areas to the detriment of his understanding of the whole. Inevitably we will do violence to these contributory disciplines if we try to do any more than to use them in our study of education. In this study, all have their part to play. To emphasize one at the expense of the others will be to give a distorted view of education of the kind we experienced in the years between the wars with the overemphasis of the psychological aspects of education theory and again in recent years through a similar concentration on its sociological aspects. Similarly, to emphasize all equally but as separate disciplines will be to lose sight of the fact that our interest in them springs only from the fact that they contribute to our understanding of education and that they cannot make this contribution in isolation from each other.

If we remember that it is education we are encouraging intending teachers to study and that we are doing this in order to improve their professional competence as teachers both in the classroom and in the wider context of education as a whole, we will provide the kind of theoretical underpinning that we are claiming is vital if teachers are to cope with the complexities of teaching in our present society.

We must not, of course, lose sight of the contribution that the study of Education through its contributory disciplines can also make to the personal education of the student nor assume that academic excellence need be confined to main studies. Many students gain great personal satisfaction from the study of Education, especially those who are able to pursue this to honours degree level, and attain a level and an appreciation of academic excellence in this way that they sometimes fail to achieve in their main subject. It is no longer possible to allocate roles to the elements of the course in this clear-cut way; we must accept the interrelationship of all elements and their varying contributions towards both the major objectives of the course. We must equally not allow this kind of consideration to tempt us into making the study of Education at the initial course level too academic for all students.

For, if the critics of the theoretical study of Education have been concerned that the attention of teachers in training has been directed here at the expense of their training in practical skills, they may have some point. We must be careful too that the requirements of new degree courses, such as the B.Ed. degree, do not lead to a further neglect of these practical skills of teaching. Students will need many basic skills and we must now turn to a consideration of their needs in this area that is growing so rapidly in importance. As we do so, it is worth noting at the very outset that this should be the focus of our initial courses, since it is in this area of professional or practical studies that all the elements of the course should meet. All should be interrelated, as we have said, and it is in the practical preparation that this interrelationship is most possible and most necessary. For this practical training must clearly have reference to the student's main studies; it must also be related to his theoretical study of education – indeed, it is difficult to establish a logical basis for distinguishing practical or professional training from this theoretical study since neither will have coherence or point without the other. Professional training, once the no man's land between main studies and Education must now be the meeting-place. This can give point to all the student's work, but again it can only do so if there is collaboration between all the tutors involved, both those concerned with the main subjects and those concerned with Education.

In the first place, 'methods' courses continue to be needed. It may be necessary, however, to extend some of them, since they must all now take cognisance of the range of abilities teachers will face in the new secondary schools and particularly in mixed-ability classes. They will need to be genuinely practical since they must offer the student as much constructive help with the job of teaching as is possible but they must also, as we continually stress, provide him with a theoretical understanding of the processes he is concerned with. They must be linked, therefore, with the study of Education and here immediately there is a need for collaboration between main subject and Education tutors. Too often students receive conflicting advice from their main subject tutors and their Education tutors and, while genuine disagreement is to be encouraged, the kind of conflict that arises from failure to communicate is clearly undesirable and can only be avoided if these tutors work together from the very outset.

In addition to such a course in the teaching of a subject, the teacher in training nowadays needs a lot more general practical preparation. It is here that he must be made aware of the new complexities of teaching, since it is these new complexities that make this additional professional provision necessary, and it is here that there has been most activity and an increase of emphasis in recent years. He needs a substantial introduction to the basic methods advocated in this book as being of value in all teaching situations but of particular value in the mixed-ability class. He needs to be introduced to the theory and the practicalities of the individual assignment, of group work in schools, of enquiry methods and of promoting creative work. If possible, he should also have an opportunity to learn something of the advantages and the problems of team-teaching. In all of these areas, but especially the latter, there is again need for collaboration between main subject tutors and Education tutors and between the main subject tutors themselves.

He will also need a lot of help in the development of specific skills. All of the skills discussed in the earlier chapters of this book are needed – skills in the teaching of slow learners, in the provision of resources of all kinds for all pupils but particularly for the non-readers or those with little reading skill, in the uses of audio-visual aids, in social education, in techniques of assessment, in careers guidance, in community service work, in the teaching of pupils from other cultures and many more. Some of these clearly will be essential for all teachers; some vital to teachers of mixed-ability classes; others perhaps can be made available as options so that teachers may be allowed to specialize in these professional areas as they can in subject areas, since here too we must avoid the jack of all trades. Again we have a strong argument for some form of team-teaching in schools so that all of these specialisms too can be made available to all pupils. In all of these areas preparation can best be undertaken if there is real collaboration between Education and main subject tutors.

Furthermore, most of these practical skills need to be developed on the job. While all of them involve a lot of theoretical work and much must be done on them in college, this must be reinforced and supported by first-hand experience in the schools. Dissatisfaction with practical preparation for teaching often stems from a lack of coordination of professional courses in college and teaching practices in the schools. Teaching practice, the fourth element in the course, must, therefore, be closely interlinked with professional courses of the kind we have been discussing. It is almost true to say that any such courses will be a waste of everybody's time if they cannot be very closely geared to school experiences the student is about to have or has just had. Unfortunately, it is easier to say this than to do it, since it is not always possible to arrange for students to have the kind of teaching practice they should have, particularly when schools are over-saturated with students. Also, it is always the case that each school is unique and the right kind of preparation for a practice in one school may be quite wrong for most others, just as the right kind of follow-up to a practice in one school will be quite wrong for most others. Here is a strong argument, therefore, for individualizing practical preparation, for ensuring that to some extent it is a preparation for a specific teaching task. One way of doing this is to involve teachers more closely in the work.

Most of what a student learns about the practicalities of teaching he learns during his periods of teaching practice. It is at this very time that his college tutors, because of their heavy commitments, can give him least time, although it is of course true that the help he does get from them at these points in his course may be highly personal and individualized. Teachers are with him in the school all the time and have a golden opportunity to give him an intense course of practical preparation for teaching tailored to his individual needs. However, if teachers are to do this job properly, they must be aware of, and, therefore, involved in the work students are doing in college. Again, we do not want to create a situation in which the bewildered student receives conflicting advice from these two sources. Nor can he be given adequate help in the school unless the advice he receives there is related to the work he has been doing in college. Again there must be collaboration. Indeed, if properly planned, this can bring about the collaboration of all concerned, the student, the teacher or teachers and all the college tutors involved and can thus lead to the practical work in school becoming a genuine focus for all the elements of the student's course. On a small scale, this has been the aim of much of the work we have been doing in recent years at Goldsmiths' College,[4] where this kind of collaborative approach to practical training has been tried in conjunction with teachers from several practice schools.

None of this will be of much value, however, if it is not further reinforced by the experiences of the student of his own course and his own education. How we teach depends to a large extent on our attitudes to education and these develop far more from our experiences of our own education than from any formal courses we may be given. Most intending teachers' attitudes to education when they enter college are determined by their school experiences. We will not change those attitudes by formal courses but only by providing them with different experiences, with the kinds of experience we hope they will try to create for their pupils. If they are to learn the value of individual assignments, they must be encouraged to undertake their own individual assignments. If they are to discover the advantages of group work, they must be given opportunities to work in groups. If they are to see the point of promoting creative work, they must be encouraged themselves to engage in creative activities. If they are to be persuaded of the need for more subtle techniques of assessment, they must be aware that we are employing such techniques in our assessment of their capabilities as teachers and that we are attempting no finer grading than is consistent with the need to ensure the maintenance of professional standards. Above all, if they are to be encouraged to develop the kinds of relationship with their pupils that we have argued as essential both to good order in a school and to the education of pupils, they must themselves experience relationships of this kind with their own teachers in college. It is in any case very difficult nowadays for tutors to adopt an authoritarian approach to their students, since all that we said in chapter 7 about the need for the teacher's authority to be based on a genuine expertise applies with even more force to the teacher in a College of Education or a University, but it is also undesirable that we should even try to adopt such an approach. We have said that teachers must learn that their difficulties are better

4 For an account of the early stages of this work see A. V. Kelly, *Ideas* no. 8/9, 1968 and A. V. Kelly and W. Davies, *University of London Institute of Education Bulletin*, Spring 1970.

solved through developing relationships than through acquiring techniques. Our students will only learn the truth of this, if they see their tutors practising it. They will also only become responsible teachers if they are treated in a responsible way.

The education and training of teachers, then, requires the development of interrelationships between all the elements of the course of training and the organizational procedures employed. If this is so, it constitutes a strong case for concurrent forms of training. Consecutive training must, of course, continue for those who wish to follow a normal degree course before committing themselves to teaching; it is right too that it should be available also to those who, while not following degree courses, want some form of higher education without first making a commitment to a career in teaching. However, we must not lose sight of the real advantages of the kind of integrated course of preparation for teaching we have endeavoured to describe and the opportunities a three- or four-year concurrent course can give for 'growing into' the profession to those who are already quite committed to it as a career. In any case, real commitment comes – or goes – only after the experience of actually teaching in a school so that the earlier students can have such experience the better.

What courses of teacher preparation must produce is teachers who have learnt to think about education and who will go on thinking about it, reading about it and discussing it with their colleagues after they have left college and throughout their professional lives, teachers who have been started off but not finished off, in either sense of the term. We must train teachers for the future rather than for the present and this means that we must promote in them the ability to adapt to and to contribute to the continuing development of educational provision. If the changes we have discussed in this book have been slow to take hold, this is due to some extent to the fact that they are having to fight against the prejudices and the closed minds that the training methods of the past have helped to create. Teachers tend to cling to their old roles in spite of changes and even where those roles are inappropriate.[5] They must be trained to welcome, initiate and thus control change. Only then can we be sure that the changes that take place will work, since teachers will only make them work if they believe in them.

Teachers must also be given opportunities to extend their expertise and bring up to date their understanding of education by regular and extensive provision for in-service training. Such provision is needed by practising teachers to give them an understanding of ongoing developments in educational theory and practice and to enable them to acquire the new skills and techniques that these developments render essential.

Furthermore, there must be continuing research and development in all areas of education. Nor must this research be too esoteric. There must be research into practical problems of the kind the Schools Council has

5 See, for example, F. Musgrove and P. H. Taylor, *Society and the Teacher's Role* (RKP, 1969), p. 71.

directed its attentions to and that universities are beginning to recognize as acceptable areas of research and enquiry. The results of this research must be made readily available to the teachers in the classrooms and the teachers themselves must be engaged as fully as possible in these projects. Opportunities should also be provided for teachers to extend their education and professional expertise by having innovations in their own work recognized as the basis of small-scale research projects which can lead to the award of a higher degree or other suitable qualification. Such a procedure would ensure that their own further study could be centred on areas relevant to their work; it would also ensure that in introducing and evaluating new developments within the school they had the advantage of guidance from tutors skilled in research methods. This is one way in which the researchers and the trainers of teachers can be brought into closer contact with the practising teachers themselves as well as with the realities of the classroom. On all fronts, there must be as much collaboration as possible between all who have a contribution to make to educational development.

If there is one lesson to be learnt from what this book has tried to say it is that there exists this need for collaboration at all levels of education and for the improved relationships that can come from collaboration of this kind. It is probably true to say that most of the things that would be generally agreed as valuable in education today are the results of successful and harmonious collaboration. It is only when pupils, teachers, parents, students, tutors, research workers, administrators and all who are concerned with education learn to work together that our schools will become the places of cooperative endeavour that institutions of learning should be. The introduction of the mixed-ability class can take us one step nearer this ideal.

Index